Applied Physics-I: Practice Questions and Answers

Applied Physics-I: Practice Questions and Answers

For Diploma Engineering Students as per AICTE new syllabus

by

Bikash Kumar Naik

Notion Press

This book is a comprehensive guide to applied physics for diploma engineering students. The content is based on the latest AICTE syllabus and is intended for educational purposes only. Any resemblance to actual textbooks, publishers, or other works is purely coincidental.

First edition, 2024

Published by Notion Press

Preface

This book, "Applied Physics-I: Practice Questions and Answers : for Diploma Engineering Students", is crafted to provide a comprehensive resource that aligns with the latest AICTE syllabus. Physics forms the foundation of engineering and technical studies, bridging concepts with real-world applications that are essential for students at the diploma level. The aim of this book is to simplify complex topics, presenting them in a clear, structured manner that promotes understanding and retention.

Each unit begins with fundamental concepts, progressing through a wide array of practice questions designed to build proficiency in both theoretical and practical aspects of applied physics. Detailed answers and step-by-step solutions are provided to encourage self-study, allowing students to review, apply, and solidify their knowledge independently. Topics covered include essential areas such as measurements, force and motion, rotational dynamics, properties of matter, and thermodynamics.

By engaging with this book, students will not only prepare themselves for exams but also gain a deeper appreciation for the role of physics in everyday engineering challenges. It is my hope that this resource serves as a valuable tool for students, fostering both confidence and skill as they advance in their studies.

Bikash Kumar Naik

Contents

Chapter I

Unit-1 : Physical World, Units and Measurements

2 Marks Questions & Solutions

- **Q1. Show that momentum and impulse have the same dimension.**
  Ans. Dimensional formula of momentum = Mass $\times$ Velocity = $[M^1L^1T^{-1}]$
  Dimensional formula of impulse = Force $\times$ Time = $[M^1L^1T^{-1}]$
  Thus, momentum and impulse have the same dimensions: $[1, 1, -1]$.

- **Q2. Write the SI unit of the following Physical quantities: (a) Power, (b) Pressure.**
  Ans.

    - SI unit of Power is Watt or Joule/second.

    - SI unit of Pressure is Pascal or N/m².

- **Q3. Convert one unit of Force from SI to CGS system.**
  Ans.

    - SI unit of Force is Newton.

    - CGS unit of Force is Dyne.

    - Force $= ma = $ Kg m/s^2
      1 Newton $=$ 1 Kg m/s^2 $=$ 1000 g $\times$ 100 cm/s^2 $=$ 10^5 g cm/s$^2 = 10^5$ Dyne.

- **Q4. The energy is expressed as $E = Kv$, where v is the velocity. Find the dimensional formula of K.**
  Ans. $E = Kv \Rightarrow [M^1L^2T^{-2}] = K[M^0L^1T^{-1}]$
  $$K = \frac{[M^1L^2T^{-2}]}{[M^0L^1T^{-1}]} = [M^1L^1T^{-1}]$$
  Dimensional formula of K is $[M^1L^1T^{-1}]$.

- **Q5. A force F is given by $F = at + bt^2$, where t is time. What is the dimensional formula of a?**

Ans. According to the principle of homogeneity,

Dimensional formula of $at =$ Dimensional formula of F

Dimensional formula of $a = \dfrac{[M^1 L^1 T^{-2}]}{[M^0 L^0 T^1]} = [M^1 L^1 T^{-3}]$.

- **Q6. If the radius of a circle is (2.0 ± 0.5) cm, then calculate the percentage error in its measurement.**

  Ans. Percentage error $= \dfrac{0.5}{2.0} \times 100 = 25\%$.

- **Q7. Error in measurement of radius of a sphere is 2%. Find the percentage error in measurement of its volume.**

  Ans. Volume of a sphere $V = \dfrac{4}{3}\pi r^3$

  Percentage error in volume $= 3 \times$ Percentage error in radius

  $= 3 \times 2\% = 6\%$.

- **Q8. Define Absolute Error.**

  Ans. Let $x_1, x_2, x_3, \ldots$ be various observations.

  $\bar{x} =$ mean of observation $= \dfrac{x_1 + x_2 + x_3 + \ldots}{n}$

  Absolute error in individual observations are $|\bar{x} - x_1|, |\bar{x} - x_2|, |\bar{x} - x_3|, \ldots$.

- **Q9. Define relative error and percentage error.**

  Ans. Relative error: It is the ratio of mean absolute error to the mean value of the observation being measured.

  Percentage error: Relative error expressed in percentage.

- **Q10. When final results involve the quotient of two measured values, $X = \dfrac{A}{B}$, what will be the expression for maximum relative error in X?**

  Ans. $\dfrac{\Delta X}{X} = \dfrac{\Delta A}{A} + \dfrac{\Delta B}{B}$

  Max. Relative error in $X =$ Max. Relative error in $A +$ Max. Relative error in B.

- **Q11. If the percentage error in momentum is 2% and the percentage error in measuring the mass of a body is 3%, find the percentage error in kinetic energy.**

  Ans. Kinetic Energy $(K) = \dfrac{1}{2}mv^2$

$$\frac{\Delta K}{K} = 2\frac{\Delta v}{v} + \frac{\Delta m}{m}$$

Percentage error of $K = 2 \times 2\% + 3\% = 7\%$.

- **Q12. Write the number of significant figures of the following: (a) 0.007 m^2 (b) 2.64×10^{24} kg (c) 0.2370 cm^{-3} (d) 0.0006032 m^2.**
  Ans. (a) 1, (b) 3, (c) 4, (d) 4.

  (a) 0.007 m^2: The number 0.007 has only one non-zero digit (7), so it has **1 significant figure**.

  (b) 2.64×10^{24} kg: In scientific notation, the number 2.64 has three digits (2, 6, and 4), and all these digits are significant. Therefore, the number 2.64×10^{24} kg has **3 significant figures**.

  (c) 0.2370 cm^{-3}: The number 0.2370 includes the digit 0 after the decimal point, which is significant because it indicates precision. Therefore, the number 0.2370 has **4 significant figures**.

  (d) 0.0006032 m^2: The number 0.0006032 has 4 significant figures because the leading zeros are not counted, and all non-zero digits (6, 0, 3, and 2) are significant. Hence, the number 0.0006032 has **4 significant figures**.

- **Q13. Convert 10 Calories into Joules.**
  Ans. 1 calorie $= 4.2$ Joules
  10 calories $= 42$ Joules.

- **Q14. Name the fundamental quantities and their units in SI.**
  Ans.

  - Mass - Kilogram

  - Length - Meter

  - Time - Second

  - Temperature - Kelvin

  - Electric Current - Ampere

  - Luminous Intensity - Candela

  - Amount of Substance - Mole

- **Q15. Two resistances $R_1 = 5.1 \pm 0.03 \ \Omega$ and $R_2 = 2.6 \pm 0.02 \ \Omega$ are connected in series in a circuit. Calculate total resistance with error limit.**

  Ans. Total resistance in series, $R = R_1 + R_2 = 5.1 + 2.6 = 7.7 \ \Omega$

  $\Delta R = \pm(\Delta R_1 + \Delta R_2) = \pm(0.03 + 0.02) = \pm 0.05$

  $R = 7.7 \pm 0.05 \ \Omega.$

- **Q16. Write the SI unit and dimensional formula of Kinetic Energy.**

  Ans. SI unit of Kinetic Energy is Joule.

  Dimensional formula of $E = \dfrac{1}{2}mv^2 = [M^1 L^2 T^{-2}].$

- **Q17. The errors in the measurement of length and breadth of a rectangular table are 3% and 2% respectively. What will be the % error in its area?**

  Ans. Given error in length $= 3\%$, error in breadth $= 2\%$.

  Since, Area $A = L \times B$

  Error in area = Error in L + Error in $B = 3\% + 2\% = 5\%.$

- **Q18. Write the dimensional formula of Force and Work.**

  Ans.

  - Force $=$ mass $\times$ acceleration $= [M^1 L^1 T^{-2}]$

  - Work $=$ Force $\times$ displacement $= [M^1 L^1 T^{-2}] \times [L^1] = [M^1 L^2 T^{-2}]$

- **Q10. The energy of a system is given by the equation $E = hf$, where E is the energy, h is Planck's constant, and f is the frequency. What are the dimensions of Planck's constant h?**

  Solution: The given equation is:

  $$E = hf$$

  Rearranging this equation to solve for h, we get:

  $$h = \frac{E}{f}$$

Dimensions of Energy (E): Energy has the dimensions of work, which is given by:

$$[E] = [M][L^2][T^{-2}]$$

where M is mass, L is length, and T is time.

Dimensions of Frequency (f): Frequency is the reciprocal of time, so the dimensions of frequency are:

$$[f] = [T^{-1}]$$

Dimensions of Planck's Constant (h): Using the equation $h = \frac{E}{f}$, we can find the dimensions of h as:

$$[h] = \frac{[E]}{[f]} = \frac{[M][L^2][T^{-2}]}{[T^{-1}]} = [M][L^2][T^{-1}]$$

Thus, the dimensions of Planck's constant h are $[ML^2T^{-1}]$.

(5 MARKS QUESTIONS & SOLUTIONS)

Q1. State the principle of homogeneity and check the correctness of the following equation:

$$E = mgh + \frac{1}{2}mv^2$$

where E = Energy, m = Mass, g = Acceleration due to gravity, v = Velocity.

Ans. The principle of homogeneity states that the dimension of each term on both sides of a correct equation must be the same.
Given,

$$E = mgh + \frac{1}{2}mv^2$$

Dimensional formula of $E = [M^1L^2T^{-2}]$
Dimensional formula of $mgh = [M^1L^2T^{-2}]$
Dimensional formula of $\frac{1}{2}mv^2 = [M^1L^2T^{-2}]$
Since the dimensional formulas of all terms in the equation are the same, the relation is dimensionally correct.

Q2. Convert one Joule of work into Ergs (CGS system).

Ans. The dimensional formula of Work $W = F \cdot s =$ Force $\times$ displacement $= [M^1 L^2 T^{-2}]$.
Given that $1\,\text{Joule} = 1\,\text{kg} \cdot \text{m}^2 \cdot \text{s}^{-2}$.
In the CGS system: $1\,\text{kg} = 1000\,\text{g}$, $1\,\text{m} = 100\,\text{cm}$, $1\,\text{s} = 1\,\text{s}$.
Thus, $1\,\text{Joule} = 1 \times 1000 \times 10^4 = 10^7$ ergs.

Q3. Using dimensional analysis, obtain an expression for the centripetal force F of a particle revolving in a horizontal circle, depending on its mass m, radius r, and velocity v.

Ans. Let us assume that the centripetal force F is given by:

$$F = k m^a r^b v^c$$

where k is a dimensionless constant, and a, b, and c are powers to be determined by dimensional analysis.

The dimensional formula for the quantities involved are:

$$\text{Force, } F : [M^1 L^1 T^{-2}]$$
$$\text{Mass, } m : [M^1]$$
$$\text{Radius, } r : [L^1]$$
$$\text{Velocity, } v : [L^1 T^{-1}]$$

Substituting these into the assumed formula for F, we have:

$$[F] = [M^1 L^1 T^{-2}] = [M^a][L^b][L^c T^{-c}]$$

Simplifying, this gives:

$$[M^a L^{b+c} T^{-c}]$$

Equating the powers of M, L, and T on both sides, we get:

$$\text{For } M : \quad a = 1$$
$$\text{For } L : \quad b + c = 1$$
$$\text{For } T : \quad -c = -2 \Rightarrow c = 2$$

Substituting $c = 2$ into $b + c = 1$, we find:

$$b = -1$$

Therefore, the values of a, b, and c are $a = 1$, $b = -1$, and $c = 2$. Substituting these into the assumed formula for F:

$$F = km^1 r^{-1} v^2 = k\frac{mv^2}{r}$$

Since k is a dimensionless constant and for centripetal force, it is generally taken as $k = 1$, we have:

$$F = \frac{mv^2}{r}$$

Q4. Given $A = \frac{a^2 c^3}{e^4}$, with percentage errors in a, c, , and e being 1%, 3%, and 2%, respectively, find the percentage error in A.

Ans. The percentage error in A is given by:

$$\text{Percentage error in } A = 2 \cdot (\text{Percentage error in } a)$$
$$+ 3 \cdot (\text{Percentage error in } c)$$
$$+ 4 \cdot (\text{Percentage error in } e).$$

Substituting the values, we get

$$\text{Percentage error in } A = (2 \cdot 1\%) + (3 \cdot 3\%) + (4 \cdot 2\%) = 19\%.$$

Q5. The time period of oscillation of a simple pendulum in an experiment is recorded as 2.56 s, 2.62 s, 2.70 s, 2.58 s, 2.45 s. Find the mean time period and the mean absolute error.

Ans. Given time periods: $T_1 = 2.56$, $T_2 = 2.62$, $T_3 = 2.70$, $T_4 = 2.58$, $T_5 = 2.45$.
Mean time period:

$$\bar{T} = \frac{2.56 + 2.62 + 2.70 + 2.58 + 2.45}{5} = 2.58 \, \text{s}$$

$$\Delta T_1 = |\bar{T} - T_1| = 0.02, \quad \Delta T_2 = 0.04, \quad \Delta T_3 = 0.12,$$

$$\Delta T_4 = 0, \quad \Delta T_5 = 0.13$$

Mean absolute error:

$$\Delta \bar{T} = \frac{\Delta T_1 + \Delta T_2 + \Delta T_3 + \Delta T_4 + \Delta T_5}{5} = \frac{0.31}{5} = 0.062 \text{ s}$$

Q6. State the principle of homogeneity. Using dimensional formula, check the correctness of the equation $v = u + at$.

Ans. The principle of homogeneity states that the dimension of each term on both sides of a correct equation must be the same.

Given $v = u + at$,

Dimensional formula of $v = [L^1 T^{-1}]$, $u = [L^1 T^{-1}]$, and $at = [L^1 T^{-1}]$.

Since all terms have the same dimensional formula, the equation is dimensionally correct.

Q7. Using dimensional formula, check the correctness of the equation $v^2 - u^2 = 2aS$.

Ans. The principle of homogeneity states that the dimension of each term on both sides of a correct equation must be the same.

Given $v^2 - u^2 = 2aS$,

Dimensional formula of $v^2 = [L^2 T^{-2}]$, $u^2 = [L^2 T^{-2}]$, and $2aS = [L^2 T^{-2}]$.

Since all terms have the same dimensional formula, the equation is dimensionally correct.

Q8. Using dimensional formula, check the correctness of the equation $S = ut + \frac{1}{2}at^2$.

Ans. According to the principle of homogeneity, all terms in a valid equation must have the same dimensions.

Given $S = ut + \frac{1}{2}at^2$,

Dimensional formula of S (displacement) is $[L]$.

Dimensional formula of ut is $[LT^{-1}] \times [T] = [L]$.

Dimensional formula of $\frac{1}{2}at^2$ is $[LT^{-2}] \times [T^2] = [L]$.

Since all terms have the same dimensional formula $[L]$, the equation is dimensionally correct.

Q9. Using dimensional analysis, obtain an expression for the time period T of a simple pendulum, depending on its length L and

acceleration due to gravity g.

Ans. Let us assume that the time period T is given by:

$$T = kL^a g^b$$

where k is a dimensionless constant, and a and b are powers to be determined by dimensional analysis.

The dimensional formula for the quantities involved are:

$$\text{Time period, } T : [T^1]$$
$$\text{Length, } L : [L^1]$$
$$\text{Acceleration due to gravity, } g : [L^1 T^{-2}]$$

Substituting these into the assumed formula for T, we have:

$$[T] = [L^a][L^b T^{-2b}]$$

Simplifying, this gives:

$$[T^1] = [L^{a+b} T^{-2b}]$$

Equating the powers of L and T on both sides, we get:

$$\text{For } L: \quad a + b = 0$$
$$\text{For } T: \quad -2b = 1 \Rightarrow b = -\frac{1}{2}$$

Substituting $b = -\frac{1}{2}$ into $a + b = 0$, we find:

$$a = \frac{1}{2}$$

Therefore, the values of a and b are $a = \frac{1}{2}$ and $b = -\frac{1}{2}$. Substituting these into the assumed formula for T:

$$T = kL^{1/2}g^{-1/2} = k\left(\frac{L}{g}\right)^{1/2}$$

Since k is a dimensionless constant and for the time period of a simple pendulum, it is generally taken as $k = 2\pi$, we have:

$$T = 2\pi\left(\frac{L}{g}\right)^{1/2}$$

Q9. The equation of a real gas is given by $\left(P + \frac{a}{V^2}\right)(V - b) = RT$. Here, P, V, and T are pressure, volume, and temperature respectively, and R is the universal gas constant. What are the dimensions of the constants a and b in this equation?

Ans: The given equation is:

$$\left(P + \frac{a}{V^2}\right)(V - b) = RT$$

Expanding the terms, we get:

$$PV - Pb + \frac{a}{V^2}V - \frac{a}{V^2}b = RT$$

Finding the dimensions of b: For the equation to be dimensionally consistent, the dimensions of $V - b$ must match the dimensions of V. Since V and $V - b$ are being added or subtracted, their dimensions must be the same.

Thus, the dimensions of b are the same as those of V:

$$[b] = [V] = [L^3]$$

Therefore, the dimensions of b are $[L^3]$, which corresponds to volume.

Finding the dimensions of a: Now, consider the term $\frac{a}{V^2}$ in the equation. For the equation to be dimensionally consistent, the dimensions of $\frac{a}{V^2}$ must match the dimensions of pressure P.

The dimensions of pressure P are:

$$[P] = [M][L^{-1}][T^{-2}]$$

The dimensions of $\frac{a}{V^2}$ are:

$$\left[\frac{a}{V^2}\right] = [P] = [M][L^{-1}][T^{-2}]$$

Therefore, the dimensions of a are:

$$[a] = [P][V^2] = [M][L^{-1}][T^{-2}][L^6] = [M][L^5][T^{-2}]$$

Thus, the dimensions of a are $[M][L^5][T^{-2}]$, which correspond to the dimensions of PV^2.

Final Answer: - The dimensions of a are $[M][L^5][T^{-2}]$, which are the same as PV^2. - The dimensions of b are $[L^3]$, which correspond to volume.

Chapter II

Unit-2 : Force & Motion

2 Marks Questions & Solutions

Q1. State parallelogram law of vector addition.
   Answer:
 Statement –
 "It states that if two vectors acting simultaneously at a point are represented in magnitude and direction by the two sides of a parallelogram drawn from that point, then their resultant is given in magnitude and direction by the diagonal of the parallelogram passing through that point."
   Mathematically,

$$\vec{R} = \vec{A} + \vec{B}$$

Q2. If $\vec{A} \cdot \vec{B} = |\vec{A} \times \vec{B}|$, then find the value of the angle between them.
   Answer:
Given $\vec{A} \cdot \vec{B} = |\vec{A} \times \vec{B}|$, we have:

$$|\vec{A}||\vec{B}| \cos\theta = |\vec{A}||\vec{B}| \sin\theta$$

Dividing both sides by $|\vec{A}||\vec{B}|$, we get:

$$\cos\theta = \sin\theta$$

which implies $\tan\theta = 1 \Rightarrow \theta = 45°$.

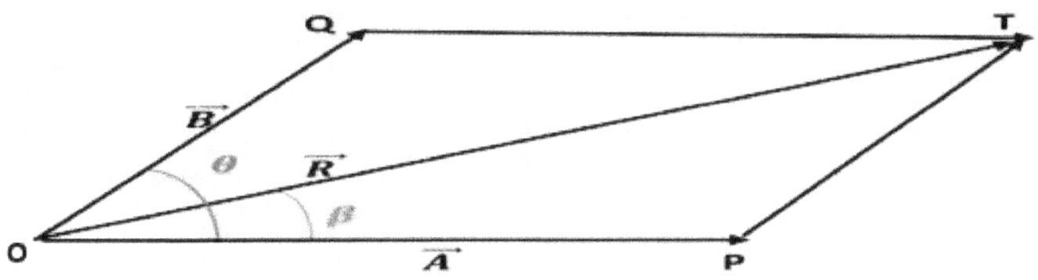

Figure II.1: parallelogram law of vector addition

Q3. If $\vec{A} = 2\hat{i} - 3\hat{k}$ and $\vec{B} = \hat{i} + 2\hat{j} - 4\hat{k}$, find $\vec{A} \times \vec{B}$.

Answer:

We use the determinant form to compute $\vec{A} \times \vec{B}$:

$$\vec{A} \times \vec{B} = \begin{vmatrix} \hat{i} & \hat{j} & \hat{k} \\ 2 & 0 & -3 \\ 1 & 2 & -4 \end{vmatrix} = \hat{i}(0 - (-6)) - \hat{j}(-(8 - 3)) + \hat{k}(4 - 0)$$

$$= 6\hat{i} + 5\hat{j} + 4\hat{k}$$

Q4. Define the Dot Product of two vectors.

Answer:

The dot product between two vectors is defined as the product of their magnitudes and the cosine of the smaller angle between them:

$$\vec{A} \cdot \vec{B} = |\vec{A}||\vec{B}| \cos \theta$$

Q5. Why does a cricket player move his hands in a backward direction while catching a ball?

Answer:

To reduce the force exerted on his hands, a cricket player moves his hands backward while catching the ball. This increases the time duration for the change in momentum, which reduces the impact force by impulse-momentum principle.

Q6. Why does a cyclist bend inward while negotiating a curved track?

Answer:

A cyclist bends inward to provide the necessary centripetal force for circular motion. Leaning inward creates a component of normal reaction that acts as the centripetal force, preventing skidding or toppling.

Q7. A ball of mass 0.1 kg strikes a wall at 30 m/s and rebounds at 20 m/s. Calculate the impulse of the force exerted.

Answer:

Given, $m = 0.1\,\text{kg}$, initial velocity $u = 30\,\text{m/s}$, final velocity $v = -20\,\text{m/s}$:

$$\text{Impulse} = m(v - u) = 0.1 \times (-20 - 30) = -5\,\text{Ns}$$

Q8. A body moves in a circular path with radius $r = 2\,\text{m}$ and angular acceleration $\alpha = 5\,\text{rad/s}^2$. Find the tangential acceleration.

Answer:

Tangential acceleration a_t is given by:

$$a_t = r\alpha = 2 \times 5 = 10 \,\text{m/s}^2$$

Q9. For what value of m, the vector $\vec{A} = 2\hat{i} + 3\hat{j} - 6\hat{k}$ is perpendicular to $\vec{B} = 3\hat{i} - m\hat{j} + 6\hat{k}$.

Answer:

Two vectors are perpendicular if their dot product is zero:

$$\vec{A} \cdot \vec{B} = 2 \times 3 + 3 \times (-m) + (-6) \times 6 = 0$$

$$6 - 3m - 36 = 0 \Rightarrow m = -10$$

Q10. A body moves in a circular path with radius $r = 3\,\text{m}$, speed $v = 9\,\text{m/s}$, and mass $m = 2\,\text{kg}$. Calculate the centripetal force.

Answer:

Centripetal Force $F = \frac{mv^2}{r}$:

$$F = \frac{2 \times 9^2}{3} = 54\,\text{N}$$

Q11. Derive the relation between linear velocity (v), angular velocity (ω), and radius (r).

Answer:

We know that:

$$\text{Linear velocity} = \frac{\text{Change in displacement}}{\text{Change in time}}$$

If Δs is the linear displacement and $\Delta\theta$ is the angular displacement over a time Δt, then:

$$v = \frac{\Delta s}{\Delta t} = r \cdot \frac{\Delta\theta}{\Delta t} = r\omega$$

Therefore, the relationship is $v = r\omega$.

Q12. Find the rectangular components of a velocity of $8\,\text{m/s}$ when one of the components makes an angle $30°$ with the resultant.

Answer:

Given, $v = 8\,\text{m/s}, \theta = 30°$:

$$\text{Component 1} = v\cos\theta = 8 \times \cos 30° = 8 \times \frac{\sqrt{3}}{2} = 4\sqrt{3}\,\text{m/s}$$

$$\text{Component 2} = v\sin\theta = 8 \times \sin 30° = 8 \times \frac{1}{2} = 4\,\text{m/s}$$

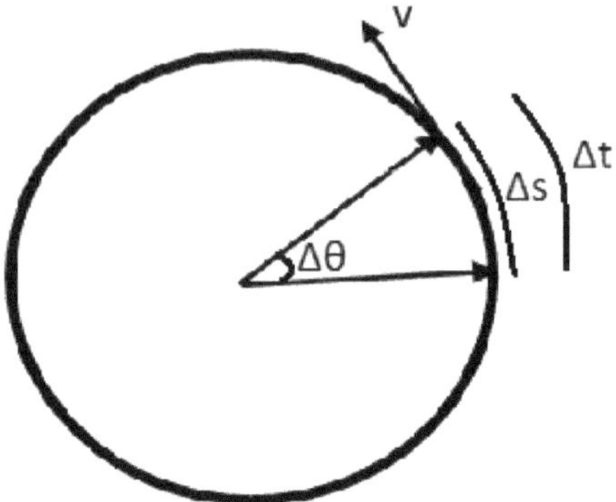

Figure II.2: linear velocity and angular velocity in circular motion

Q13. Define centripetal and centrifugal forces.

Answer:

Centripetal Force: This is the force required to move a body uniformly in a circle, directed towards the center along the radius.

Centrifugal Force: This is a pseudo force that appears to act on a body moving in a circular path, directed away from the center of rotation.

Q14. State triangle law of vector addition.

Answer:

Statement - If two vectors are represented in magnitude and direction by two sides of a triangle taken in the same order, then their resultant is represented in magnitude and direction by the third side of the triangle taken in the opposite order.

$$\vec{R} = \vec{A} + \vec{B}$$

Q15. Explain the basic concepts of rocket propulsion.

Answer:

Fuel and oxygen burn in the ignition chamber, producing hot gases that escape from the rear opening. According to the conservation of momentum, as the gases are expelled backward, the rocket gains forward momentum, propelling it forward.

Q16. A ball of mass 160 g exerts a force of 5 N on the hands of a cricketer for 20 s. Find the impulse.

Answer:

Given: $m = 160\,\text{g} = 0.16\,\text{kg}, F = 5\,\text{N}, t = 20\,\text{s}$:

$$\text{Impulse} = F \times t = 5 \times 20 = 100\,\text{Ns}$$

Q17. What will be the maximum and minimum values of the magnitude of the resultant of two vectors $\vec{A}$ and $\vec{B}$?

Answer:

Maximum Value = $|\vec{A}| + |\vec{B}|$

Minimum Value = $|\vec{A}| - |\vec{B}|$

Q18. What is the relation between time period and frequency of a body moving in a circular path?

Answer:

The relation between time period T and frequency f is:

$$f = \frac{1}{T}$$

where T is the time taken for one complete revolution and f is the number of revolutions per unit time.

5 Marks Questions & Solutions

Q:1 What is the necessity of banking the roads? What are the factors upon which the angle of banking of a road depends? A circular track of radius 600 m is to be designed for cars moving at an average speed of 180 km/h. What should be the angle of banking of the track? (Take $g = 10\,\text{m/s}^2$)

Ans:

Necessity of banking the roads: As an automobile negotiates a curve, it requires a centripetal force. The frictional force between the ground and the tyres is often insufficient to provide this force. Therefore, the outer edge of the road is raised above the inner edge to generate an additional component of force that supplies the necessary centripetal force.

Angle of banking depends upon:

1. Velocity of the vehicle.

2. Radius of curvature of the curve.

The angle of banking θ is given by:

$$\tan\theta = \frac{v^2}{rg}$$

Solution:

Given:

$$r = 600\,\text{m}, \quad v = 180\,\text{km/h} = 50\,\text{m/s}, \quad g = 10\,\text{m/s}^2$$

$$\theta = \tan^{-1}\left(\frac{50 \times 50}{600 \times 10}\right)$$

$$\theta = \tan^{-1}\left(\frac{2500}{6000}\right) = \tan^{-1}(0.4167)$$

$$\theta \approx 22.6°$$

Q:2 State and prove the principle of conservation of linear momentum.

A: In an isolated system (no external force), the total linear momentum remains conserved. From Newton's 2nd law:

$$\vec{F} = \frac{d\vec{p}}{dt} = \frac{d(m\vec{v})}{dt}$$

For an isolated system:

$$\vec{F} = 0 \Rightarrow \frac{d\vec{p}}{dt} = 0 \Rightarrow \vec{p} = \text{constant}$$

Hence, the total linear momentum before and after any event in an isolated system remains constant.

Q:3 Why is it easier to pull a lawn roller than to push it?

A: Consider a lawn roller of weight W pulled or pushed by a force $\vec{F}$ making an angle θ with the horizontal.

- When pushing: The horizontal force $F\cos\theta$ moves the roller forward, but the effective weight increases to $W + F\sin\theta$, making it harder to push.

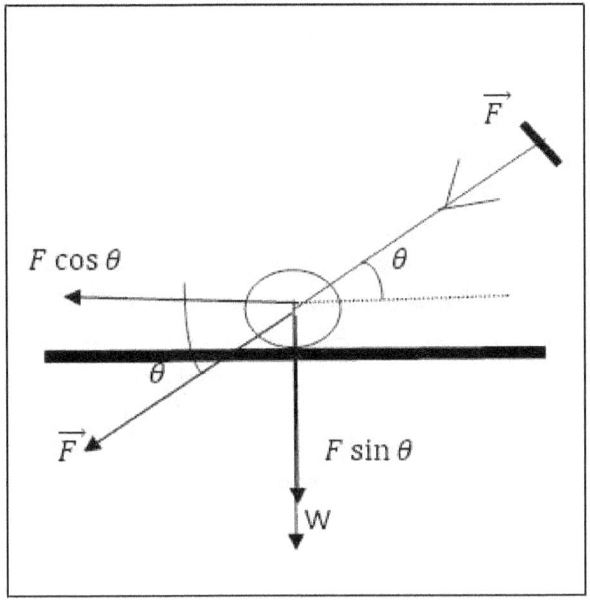

Figure II.3: Push

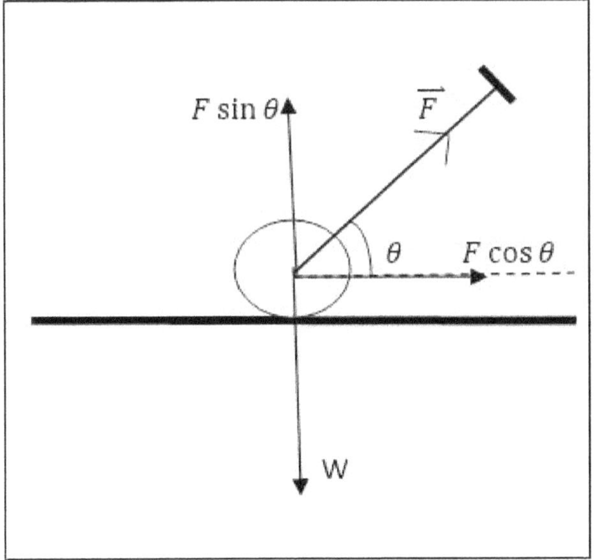

Figure II.4: Pull

- When pulling: The horizontal force $F\cos\theta$ still moves the roller forward, but the effective weight reduces to $W - F\sin\theta$, making it easier to pull.

Q:4 Derive the expression for the recoil velocity of a gun using conservation of linear momentum.

A: Consider a gun of mass M firing a bullet of mass m with velocity u. The gun recoils with velocity v.

$$\text{Before firing:} \quad \text{Momentum} = 0$$

$$\text{After firing:} \quad \text{Momentum} = mu + Mv$$

By conservation of linear momentum:

$$0 = mu + Mv \Rightarrow v = -\frac{mu}{M}$$

The negative sign indicates the gun moves in the opposite direction of the bullet.

Q:5 At what angle should two forces $F_1 = A + B$ and $F_2 = A - B$ be inclined to result in $A + B$ as the resultant?

Solution:

Let the two forces be represented as:

$$F_1 = A + B, \quad F_2 = A - B.$$

We are tasked with finding the angle between these two forces such that their resultant is $A + B$.

Step 1: Expression for the resultant force

The magnitude of the resultant of two forces F_1 and F_2 can be found using the formula:

$$R = \sqrt{F_1^2 + F_2^2 + 2F_1F_2\cos\theta},$$

where R is the magnitude of the resultant force, and θ is the angle between the forces.

Step 2: Substitute the values of F_1 and F_2

Substituting $F_1 = A + B$ and $F_2 = A - B$ into the formula for the resultant:

$$R = \sqrt{(A+B)^2 + (A-B)^2 + 2(A+B)(A-B)\cos\theta}.$$

Step 3: Simplify the expression

Now, expand and simplify the terms inside the square root:

$$R = \sqrt{(A^2 + 2AB + B^2) + (A^2 - 2AB + B^2) + 2(A^2 - B^2)\cos\theta}.$$

Simplify further:

$$R = \sqrt{2A^2 + 2B^2 + 2(A^2 - B^2)\cos\theta}.$$

Step 4: Set the resultant equal to $A + B$

We are given that the resultant should be equal to $A + B$. Thus, we set $R = A + B$:

$$A + B = \sqrt{2A^2 + 2B^2 + 2(A^2 - B^2)\cos\theta}.$$

Now, square both sides:

$$(A + B)^2 = 2A^2 + 2B^2 + 2(A^2 - B^2)\cos\theta.$$

Expand both sides:

$$A^2 + 2AB + B^2 = 2A^2 + 2B^2 + 2(A^2 - B^2)\cos\theta.$$

Step 5: Solve for $\cos\theta$

Now, rearrange the equation to isolate $\cos\theta$:

$$2AB = A^2 + B^2 + 2(A^2 - B^2)\cos\theta.$$

Solve for $\cos\theta$:

$$2(A^2 - B^2)\cos\theta = 2AB - A^2 - B^2,$$

$$\cos\theta = \frac{2AB - A^2 - B^2}{2(A^2 - B^2)}.$$

Step 6: Final answer

Thus, the angle θ between the forces is given by:

$$\theta = \cos^{-1}\left(\frac{2AB - A^2 - B^2}{2(A^2 - B^2)}\right).$$

This is the required angle for which the two forces F_1 and F_2 will result in $A + B$ as the resultant.

Q:6 The ratio of the magnitudes of two forces is 3:5, and the magnitude of their resultant is 35 N. If they are inclined at 60°, find their individual magnitudes.

A: Let $A = 3x$ and $B = 5x$, where $R = 35\,\text{N}$ and $\theta = 60°$.

$$R^2 = A^2 + B^2 + 2AB \cos \theta$$

$$35^2 = (3x)^2 + (5x)^2 + 2(3x)(5x) \cos 60°$$

$$1225 = 49x^2 \Rightarrow x = 5$$

Thus, $A = 15\,\text{N}$ and $B = 25\,\text{N}$.

Q7. Derive the rocket equation and explain its significance in the context of rocket propulsion.

Solution:

Consider a rocket moving in space, where: - v is the velocity of the rocket, - $m(t)$ is the mass of the rocket at time t, - v_e is the velocity of the exhaust gases relative to the rocket, - $\dot{m}$ is the rate at which fuel is expelled from the rocket (with $\dot{m} = -\frac{dm}{dt}$).

According to Newton's second law, the force on the rocket is the rate of change of momentum. The momentum of the rocket and the fuel together is given by:

$$F = \frac{d}{dt}(m(t)v)$$

This can be written as:

$$F = m(t)\frac{dv}{dt} + v\frac{dm(t)}{dt}$$

Now, the force on the rocket is also caused by the expulsion of fuel, and the thrust force is given by:

$$F = \dot{m}v_e$$

Equating the two expressions for the force:

$$m(t)\frac{dv}{dt} + v\frac{dm(t)}{dt} = -\dot{m}v_e$$

Since $\dot{m} = \frac{dm}{dt}$, we can rewrite the equation as:

$$m(t)\frac{dv}{dt} + v\dot{m} = -\dot{m}v_e$$

Rearranging to isolate $\frac{dv}{dt}$:

$$m(t)\frac{dv}{dt} = -\dot{m}(v_e - v)$$

If we take the reference frame in which v is small compared to v_e, or consider v at the instant of fuel expulsion, we have:

$$m(t)\frac{dv}{dt} = -\dot{m}v_e$$

This simplifies to:

$$\frac{dv}{dt} = -\frac{\dot{m}v_e}{m(t)}$$

To find the velocity change, integrate both sides of the equation:

$$\int_0^v dv = -v_e \int_{m_0}^m \frac{dm}{m}$$

After integrating, we get:

$$v = v_e \ln\left(\frac{m_0}{m}\right)$$

Where: - m_0 is the initial mass of the rocket (including fuel), - m is the mass of the rocket at any time t, - v_e is the effective exhaust velocity.

The final form of the rocket equation is:

$$\Delta v = v_e \ln\left(\frac{m_0}{m_f}\right)$$

where Δv is the change in velocity, and m_f is the final mass of the rocket after fuel is expelled.

Significance:

This equation is important because it shows how a rocket moves by expelling fuel at high speed. The rocket's change in velocity depends on the ratio of the initial mass to the final mass and the exhaust velocity. Practically, this means rockets need a lot of fuel to achieve even a small speed increase.

Q.8. Two forces $F_1 = P + Q$ and $F_2 = P - Q$ are acting on a point. If the resultant force is given by $F = \sqrt{3P^2 + Q^2}$, at what angle should these two forces be inclined to each other so as to produce the given resultant?

Solution:

Let the two forces be $F_1 = P + Q$ and $F_2 = P - Q$, and let the resultant force be $F = \sqrt{3P^2 + Q^2}$.

According to the parallelogram law of vector addition, the magnitude of the resultant force F is given by:

$$F^2 = F_1^2 + F_2^2 + 2F_1 F_2 \cos\theta$$

Substitute the values of F_1 and F_2:

$$F^2 = (P + Q)^2 + (P - Q)^2 + 2(P + Q)(P - Q)\cos\theta$$

Now, expand the terms:

$$F^2 = (P^2 + 2PQ + Q^2) + (P^2 - 2PQ + Q^2) + 2(P^2 - Q^2)\cos\theta$$

Simplify the expression:

$$F^2 = 2P^2 + 2Q^2 + 2(P^2 - Q^2)\cos\theta$$

We are given that the resultant $F = \sqrt{3P^2 + Q^2}$, so substitute this into the equation:

$$(\sqrt{3P^2 + Q^2})^2 = 2P^2 + 2Q^2 + 2(P^2 - Q^2)\cos\theta$$

Simplify:

$$3P^2 + Q^2 = 2P^2 + 2Q^2 + 2(P^2 - Q^2)\cos\theta$$

Now, collect like terms:

$$3P^2 + Q^2 - 2P^2 - 2Q^2 = 2(P^2 - Q^2)\cos\theta$$

Simplify:

$$P^2 - Q^2 = 2(P^2 - Q^2)\cos\theta$$

Solving for $\cos\theta$:

$$\cos\theta = \frac{1}{2}$$

Thus, the angle θ is:

$$\theta = \cos^{-1}\left(\frac{1}{2}\right) = 60°$$

The angle between the two forces should be $60°$ to produce the given resultant.

Chapter III

Unit III: Work, Power and Energy

2 Marks Questions & Solutions

Q-1: Define work done and write its SI unit & CGS unit.
Ans: Work done can be defined as the dot product of force and displacement:

$$W = \vec{F} \cdot \vec{r}$$

SI unit of work done is joule (J) and CGS unit is erg.

Q-2: Write the conditions for zero work done.
Ans:

- When applied force $(F) = 0$

- When net displacement $(r) = 0$

- When applied force is perpendicular to displacement, i.e., $\theta = 90°$

Q-3: Write any two examples of Zero work.
Ans:

- Work done when walking forward while lifting some object

- Work done when a moving car is stopped by applying brakes

Q-4:Give two examples of negative work done.
Ans:

- Friction force acting on a rolling ball in opposite direction to displacement.

- Force due to gravity acting on a ball thrown vertically upwards.

Q-5: Write any two examples of positive work.
Ans:

- Work done by force due to gravity acting on a ball falling to the ground.

- Work done by a crane or helicopter lifting heavy objects from the ground.

Q-6:Give a comparison between positive work done and negative work done.

Ans:

- Positive work done: When the applied force is parallel to displacement $(\theta = 0°)$, $W = +F \cdot S$.

- Negative work done: When the applied force is anti-parallel to displacement $(\theta = 180°)$, $W = -F \cdot S$.

Q-7: A porter uses a 50 N force to lift a luggage bag and walks forward to cover 100 m of displacement. Calculate the amount of work done by the porter.

Ans: Given $F = 50\,\text{N}$ and $S = 100\,\text{m}$, we observe that $\theta = 90°$. We know:

$$W = F \cdot S \cdot \cos(\theta) = 50 \times 100 \times \cos(90°) = 0\,\text{J}$$

Q-8: Define friction and write its dimensional formula.

Ans: Friction is an opposing force that acts in the opposite direction of the applied force when a body moves or tends to move on a surface. The dimensional formula of friction is:

$$[M^1 L^1 T^{-2}]$$

Q-9:Explain static friction with a figure.

Ans: Static friction comes into play when the object is in contact with the surface and force is applied on the object. Static friction exists between two surfaces until the object starts to move by the application of force. The direction of static friction is opposite to the applied force.

Q-10: Define the coefficient of friction.

Ans: The coefficient of friction is the ratio of the magnitude of limiting friction to the normal reaction. It is a unitless, dimensionless physical quantity:

$$\mu = \frac{F_{\text{lim}}}{N}$$

Q-11: Define energy and write its SI and CGS units.

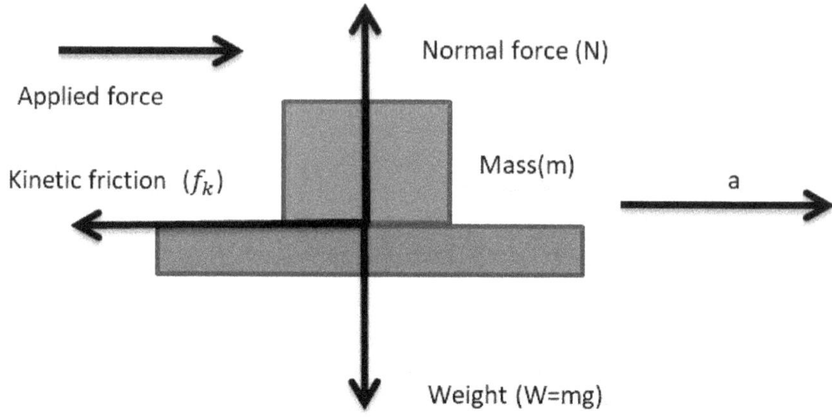

Figure III.1: Work done against friction on a horizontal surface.

Ans: Energy is the ability to do work. It is a scalar quantity. SI unit of energy is joule (J) or N.m, and CGS unit is erg or dyne.cm.

Q-12: List out various types of friction with examples.
Ans:

- **Static friction:** It opposes motion when there is no relative motion between the surfaces. Example: Applying a small amount of force to move a heavy box.

- **Kinetic or dynamic friction:**

  - **Sliding friction:** Opposes motion when one surface slides over another. Example: Pushing a machine on the floor.

  - **Rolling friction:** Opposes motion when one surface rolls over another. Example: Rolling of a wheel or ball.

Q-13:What is meant by the conservation of energy?
Ans: No energy can be created or destroyed; it can only change from one form to another. For example, when a car slips down a slanted road, the potential energy is converted into kinetic energy, and as the car slows down, the kinetic energy is transformed into thermal energy.

Q-14: Compare kinetic energy and gravitational potential energy with examples.

Ans:

- **Kinetic energy (KE):** The ability of a moving object to do work. For an object of mass m moving with velocity v, the kinetic energy is:

$$KE = \frac{1}{2}mv^2$$

Example: Bullet fired from a gun.

- **Gravitational Potential Energy (PE):** The energy stored in an object due to its position in a gravitational field. For an object of mass m at height h, the potential energy is:

$$PE = mgh$$

Example: An apple on a tree before it falls.

Q-15: A machine raises a load of 750 N through a height of 16 m in 5 seconds. Calculate the power at which the machine works.

Ans: Given force $F = 750\,\text{N}$, displacement $h = 16\,\text{m}$, and time $t = 5\,\text{s}$, the work done by the machine is:

$$W = F \cdot h = 750 \times 16 = 12000\,\text{J}$$

The power of the machine is:

$$P = \frac{W}{t} = \frac{12000}{5} = 2400\,\text{W}$$

Q-16: Give two examples of transformation of energy.

Ans:

- Electric energy to heat energy: Water heater, room heater.

- Solar energy to electric energy: Solar cells or photovoltaic cells.

Q-17: Define power with an example. Write its SI unit.

Ans: Power is the rate at which work is done or energy is transferred. The SI unit of power is watt (W), which is equivalent to J/S. Example: The power of muscles is shown by how fast you climb a mountain.

Q-18: What energy transformations take place in the following situations?

1. **When an electric bulb is switched on.**

2. **At a thermal power station.**

Ans.

- (a) When an electric bulb is switched on: Electric energy changes into light and heat energy.

- (b) At a thermal power station: Heat energy is converted into electrical energy.

Q-19: Derive the relation of power with a constant force and velocity.
Ans: Instantaneous power is defined as:

$$P = \frac{W}{t} = \frac{F \cdot S}{t}$$

For constant force F and velocity v, this becomes:

$$P = F \cdot v$$

Q-20: A 2 kg body free falls from rest from a height of 12 m. Determine the work done by the force of gravity and the change in gravitational potential energy. Consider $g = 10\,\text{m/s}^2$.
Ans: Work done by gravity is:

$$W = mgh = 2 \times 12 \times 10 = 240\,\text{J}$$

The change in gravitational potential energy is also 240 J as the body falls from a height.

Q-21: A block of mass 5 kg is pulled by a constant force of 10 N on a frictionless surface. Find the work done by the force when the block moves through a distance of 20 meters.
Ans: The work done by the force is given by:

$$W = F \cdot d$$

where $F = 10\,\text{N}$ and $d = 20\,\text{m}$, so:

$$W = 10 \times 20 = 200\,\text{J}$$

(5 Marks Questions & Solutions)

Q-1 Define limiting friction and state laws of limiting friction.

Ans: Limiting friction is the maximum value of static friction that resists the relative motion between two surfaces in contact. It occurs when an external force applied to an object just starts to overcome the frictional force, causing the object to begin moving.

Laws of Limiting Friction:

1. The direction of limiting friction is always opposite to the direction of motion and it acts tangentially to the surface.

2. It depends on the nature and the state of polish of the surfaces in contact.

3. The magnitude of limiting friction is directly proportional to the magnitude of the normal reaction of the body.

4. It is independent of the shape and size of the body, as long as the normal reaction remains the same.

Q-2 Write methods to reduce friction.

Ans:

1. **Rubbing or Polishing surfaces:** Making the surfaces smooth by rubbing or polishing can reduce friction.

2. **Use of ball bearings:** Using ball bearings between moving parts can reduce friction and allow smooth movement.

3. **Using lubricants:** Lubricating machinery parts with oil, grease, etc., can create a thin layer between surfaces to reduce friction.

4. **Make the object streamlined:** Streamlining the shape of the object can reduce friction.

5. **Converting sliding friction into rolling friction:** By using rolling friction instead of sliding friction, the frictional force can be reduced.

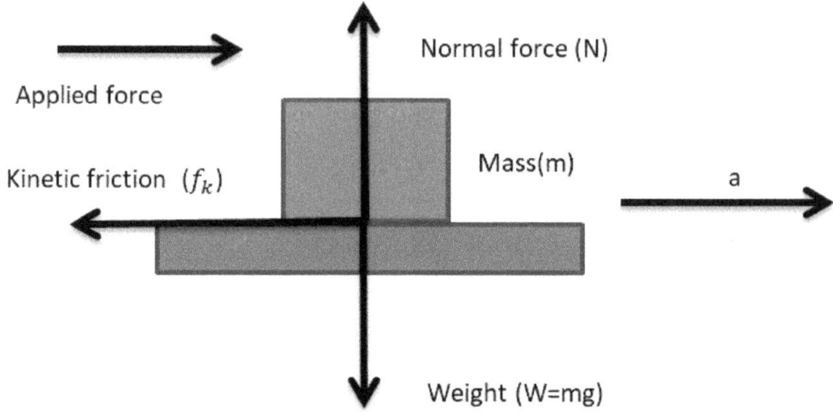

Figure III.2: Work done against friction on a horizontal surface.

Q-3 Find an expression for the work done against friction when a body is moving on a horizontal plane.

Ans: Let a block of mass m be placed on a horizontal table. The normal force acting upwards cancels out the weight of the block acting downwards. If a force is applied to move the block, friction will oppose the motion.

The kinetic friction f_k can be expressed as:

$$f_k = \mu_k N = \mu_k mg$$

where μ_k is the coefficient of kinetic friction and $N = mg$ is the normal force. The work done against friction is given by:

$$W = \vec{F} \cdot \vec{d} = f_k d \cos\theta$$

Since the direction of friction is opposite to the direction of motion ($\theta = 180°$), we have:

$$W = -f_k d = -\mu_k mgd$$

This is the expression for the work done against friction.

Q-4 Derive the expression for gravitational potential energy in moving an object of mass m from infinity to the surface of the Earth.

Ans: Let the mass of the Earth be M and the radius of the Earth be R. The work done by the gravitational force in moving a mass m from infinity to the

Figure III.3: Gravitational potential energy in moving an object of mass m from infinity to the surface of the Earth

surface of the Earth is given by:

$$W = \int_{\infty}^{R} F(x)\, dx$$

where $F(x) = \frac{GMm}{x^2}$ is the gravitational force between the Earth and the test mass m.

Thus, the work done is:

$$W = \int_{\infty}^{R} \frac{GMm}{x^2}\, dx$$

Solving the integral:

$$W = GMm \left(-\frac{1}{R} + \frac{1}{\infty} \right) = -\frac{GMm}{R}$$

The work done by the gravitational force is stored as gravitational potential energy:

$$U = -\frac{GMm}{R}$$

Q-5 Explain the conservation of mechanical energy for a freely falling body.

Ans: The conservation of mechanical energy states that the total mechanical energy (sum of kinetic and potential energy) remains constant for a freely falling body under the influence of gravity.

Given:

- $g = 9.8\,\text{m/s}^2$, the acceleration due to gravity.

- The object is initially at point A with a height H from the ground.

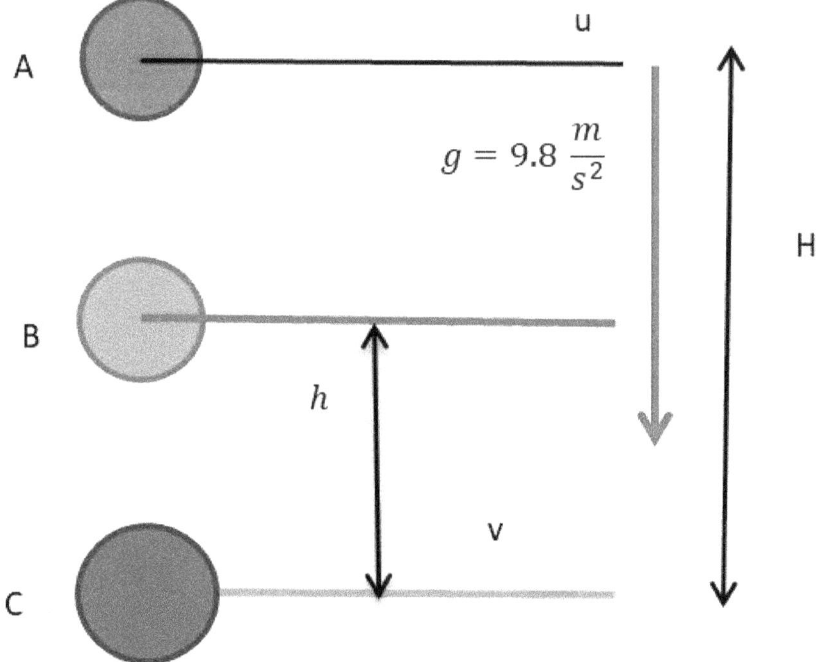

Figure III.4: Conservation of Mechanical Energy for a Freely Falling Body.

- The object passes point B, a distance h above the ground.

- When the object reaches point C, it has fallen the entire height H.

1. At Point A:

$$\text{Initial velocity} \quad u = 0,$$

$$\text{Height from the ground} \quad H.$$

Mechanical energy at point A: $\quad E_A = \text{K.E.} + \text{P.E.} = 0 + mgH = mgH.$

2. At Point B:

The object has fallen a distance (H - h), so its potential energy is mgh.

Let v be the velocity of the object at point B.

Mechanical energy at point B: $\quad E_B = \frac{1}{2}mv^2 + mgh.$

Using the equation of motion:

$$v^2 = u^2 + 2g(H - h)$$

Since $u = 0$,

$$v^2 = 2g(H - h).$$

Substituting v^2 into the expression for E_B:

$$E_B = \frac{1}{2}m \cdot 2g(H - h) + mgh = mg(H - h) + mgh = mgH.$$

3. At Point C:

The object has reached the ground, so $h = 0$.

Let v_f be the final velocity at point C.

Mechanical energy at point C: $\quad E_C = \frac{1}{2}mv_f^2 + 0.$

Using the equation of motion:

$$v_f^2 = 2gH.$$

Therefore:

$$E_C = \frac{1}{2}m \cdot 2gH = mgH.$$

Thus, the total mechanical energy remains constant as the body falls, confirming the conservation of mechanical energy:

$$E_A = E_B = E_C = mgH.$$

Q-6: A volleyball player applies a force of 24 N on a volleyball, making angles of:

1. **30° with the horizontal plane,**

2. **45° with the horizontal plane,**

3. **60° with the horizontal plane.**

The work done on the ball is 2500 J in all cases. Find the displacement of the ball in each case.

Ans.:

We know that the work done W on an object is given by the formula:

$$W = F \cdot d \cdot \cos(\theta)$$

where: - $F = 24\,\text{N}$ is the force applied, - d is the displacement of the ball, - θ is the angle between the force and the displacement.

Given that the work done is 2500 J in all cases, we can rearrange the formula to solve for d:

$$d = \frac{W}{F \cdot \cos(\theta)}$$

Now, we calculate the displacement for each case:

1. **When $\theta = 30°$:**

$$d = \frac{2500}{24 \cdot \cos(30°)}$$

Using $\cos(30°) = \frac{\sqrt{3}}{2}$:

$$d = \frac{2500}{24 \cdot \frac{\sqrt{3}}{2}} = \frac{2500}{12\sqrt{3}} \approx \frac{2500}{20.7846} \approx 120.1\,\text{m}$$

2. **When $\theta = 45°$:**

$$d = \frac{2500}{24 \cdot \cos(45°)}$$

Using $\cos(45°) = \frac{\sqrt{2}}{2}$:

$$d = \frac{2500}{24 \cdot \frac{\sqrt{2}}{2}} = \frac{2500}{12\sqrt{2}} \approx \frac{2500}{16.9706} \approx 147.2\,\text{m}$$

3. **When $\theta = 60°$:**

$$d = \frac{2500}{24 \cdot \cos(60°)}$$

Using $\cos(60°) = \frac{1}{2}$:

$$d = \frac{2500}{24 \cdot \frac{1}{2}} = \frac{2500}{12} \approx 208.3\,\text{m}$$

Answer:

1. The displacement when the angle is 30° is approximately 120.1 m.

2. The displacement when the angle is 45° is approximately 147.2 m.

3. The displacement when the angle is 60° is approximately 208.3 m.

Chapter IV

Unit-IV : Rotational Motion

2 Marks Questions and Solutions

1. **Define Torque.**

   - Torque is defined as the force that causes an object to rotate about an axis. It is also known as the moment of force.

   - Mathematically, torque $\vec{\tau}$ is given by:

   $$\vec{\tau} = \vec{r} \times \vec{F}$$

   where $\vec{r}$ is the position vector of the point of application of the force and $\vec{F}$ is the applied force.

2. **Define angular momentum.**

   - Angular momentum is a vector quantity that describes the rotational motion of a particle or system of particles. It is the rotational analog of linear momentum.

   - Mathematically, angular momentum $\vec{L}$ is given by:

   $$\vec{L} = \vec{r} \times \vec{p} = \vec{r} \times m\vec{v}$$

   where $\vec{r}$ is the position vector, $\vec{v}$ is the velocity, and m is the mass of the particle.

3. **State the principle of conservation of angular momentum.**

   - The principle of conservation of angular momentum states that if the net external torque on a body is zero, then its angular momentum remains constant.

   - Mathematically, if $\vec{\tau}_{\text{ext}} = 0$, then:

   $$\vec{L} = \text{constant}$$

4. **Define moment of inertia.**

   - Moment of inertia is a measure of the rotational inertia of a body. It quantifies the resistance of a body to change its rotational speed about an axis.

   - It is given by:

   $$I = mr^2$$

   where m is the mass of a particle and r is the perpendicular distance of the particle from the axis of rotation.

5. **State the factors on which the moment of inertia of a body depends.**

   - The moment of inertia depends on the following factors:
     - Distribution of mass about the axis of rotation.
     - Shape of the body.
     - Position and orientation of the axis of rotation with respect to the body.

6. **What is the real-world significance of the moment of inertia?**

   - The moment of inertia is crucial in real-world applications because it determines how easily an object can be rotated.

   - It plays an essential role in the design of machines and structures involving rotational motion, such as turbines, flywheels, aircraft, and ships.

7. **Write two applications of conservation of angular momentum.**

   - The angular momentum of planets remains conserved as they revolve around the sun.

   - Ice skaters use the conservation of angular momentum to change their angular velocity by adjusting their moment of inertia.

8. **The angular speed of a planet increases when its position in the orbit is near the sun. Explain why?**

- As the planet moves closer to the sun, its moment of inertia decreases. To conserve angular momentum, the angular speed increases.

$$I\omega = \text{constant}$$

9. **Derive the relation between angular momentum and moment of inertia for a mass m rotated about an axis of rotation in a circle of radius r.**

   - For a particle of mass m moving in a circle of radius r with angular velocity ω, the angular momentum L is:

   $$L = rp = mvr = mr^2\omega$$

   where $p = mv$ is the linear momentum.

   - The moment of inertia of the particle is $I = mr^2$, so we can write:

   $$L = I\omega$$

10. **Define Rotational Motion with examples.**

    - Rotational motion occurs when a rigid body rotates about a fixed axis such that each particle of the body moves in a circle around the axis of rotation.

    - Examples include the motion of wheels, gears, motors, and the blades of a helicopter.

11. **The moment of inertia of a ring about an axis passing through its center and perpendicular to its plane is MR^2. Find the moment of inertia about its diameter.**

    - Using the Perpendicular Axis Theorem, the moment of inertia about an axis perpendicular to the plane is the sum of the moments of inertia about two perpendicular axes in the plane.

    $$I_Z = I_X + I_Y$$

    - The moment of inertia about the center is $I_Z = MR^2$. Therefore, the moment of inertia about the diameter is:

    $$I_X = I_Y = \frac{I_Z}{2} = \frac{1}{2}MR^2$$

12. **The moment of inertia of a body is 5 kg m^2. Calculate the torque required for producing an angular acceleration of 2 rad/s^2.**

    - Torque is given by:

    $$\tau = I\alpha = 5 \times 2 = 10\,\text{N m}$$

13. **Deduce the moment of inertia for the solid sphere of mass 5 kg and radius 2 m about an axis tangent to its surface.**

    - The moment of inertia of a solid sphere about its center is:

    $$I_{\text{center}} = \frac{2}{5}MR^2$$

    - Using the Parallel Axis Theorem, the moment of inertia about an axis tangent to the surface is:

    $$I_{\text{tangent}} = I_{\text{center}} + MR^2 = \frac{2}{5}MR^2 + MR^2 = \frac{7}{5}MR^2$$

    - Substituting $M = 5\,\text{kg}$ and $R = 2\,\text{m}$:

    $$I_{\text{tangent}} = \frac{7}{5} \times 5 \times (2)^2 = 28\,\text{kg m}^2$$

14. **Mass of a ring is 20 g and radius is 5 cm. Calculate the momentum of inertia of the ring about its diameter.**

    - The moment of inertia of the ring about its diameter is:

    $$I = \frac{1}{2}MR^2$$

    - Substituting $M = 20\,\text{g} = 0.02\,\text{kg}$ and $R = 5\,\text{cm} = 0.05\,\text{m}$:

    $$I = \frac{1}{2} \times 0.02 \times (0.05)^2 = 1.25 \times 10^{-4}\,\text{kg m}^2$$

15. **Find the radius of gyration of a solid uniform sphere of radius R about its tangent.**

    - The moment of inertia of a solid uniform sphere about its tangent is:

    $$I = \frac{7}{5}MR^2$$

- The radius of gyration K is given by:

$$I = MK^2 \quad \Rightarrow \quad K^2 = \frac{7}{5}R^2 \quad \Rightarrow \quad K = \sqrt{\frac{7}{5}}R$$

16. **Write SI unit and dimensional formula of Moment of Inertia.**

   - SI Unit: kg m^2

   - Dimensional Formula: $[ML^2T^0]$

17. **During tornado, angular speed of air is very large. Explain why?**

   - In a tornado, as the air moves towards the center, its moment of inertia decreases. To conserve angular momentum, its angular speed increases.

18. **Define translational motion with examples.**

   - Translational motion occurs when every particle of the body moves in the same direction with the same velocity.

   - Examples include a car moving in a straight line and a bullet fired from a gun.

19. **Define angular acceleration of a body. Write its SI unit.**

   - Angular acceleration is the rate of change of angular velocity with respect to time.

   - SI Unit: rad/s^2

20. **Write SI unit and dimensional formula of torque.**

   - SI Unit: N m

   - Dimensional Formula: $[ML^2T^{-2}]$

21. **Calculate the torque about the origin for force $\vec{F} = mg\hat{j}$ and $\vec{r} = x\hat{i} + y\hat{j}$.**

   - The torque is given by:

$$\vec{\tau} = \vec{r} \times \vec{F} = (x\hat{i} + y\hat{j}) \times mg\hat{j} = mgx\hat{k}$$

22. **Write SI unit and dimensional formula of radius of gyration.**

    - SI Unit: meter

    - Dimensional Formula: $[M^0 L T^0]$

23. **Why is the moment of inertia of a body always referred to as about an axis?**

    - The moment of inertia depends on the axis of rotation, as the distance of particles from the axis changes with the axis's position. Therefore, it is always referred to as about a specific axis.

24. **A flywheel has a moment of inertia of 2×10^4 kg m^2 about its axis. Determine its kinetic energy when it rotates with an angular velocity of 2.5 rad/s.**

    - The kinetic energy is given by:

$$KE = \frac{1}{2} I \omega^2 = \frac{1}{2} \times 2 \times 10^4 \times (2.5)^2 = 6.25 \times 10^4 \, \text{J}$$

25. **A ring has a mass of 0.05 kg and radius 0.05 m. What will be its moment of inertia about an axis passing through its center and perpendicular to its plane?**

    - The moment of inertia is given by:

$$I = MR^2 = 0.05 \times (0.05)^2 = 1.25 \times 10^{-4} \, \text{kg m}^2$$

26. **State the Perpendicular Axis Theorem of M.I.**

    - The Perpendicular Axis Theorem states that for a planar lamina, the moment of inertia about an axis perpendicular to the plane is equal to the sum of the moments of inertia about two perpendicular axes in the plane, which intersect at a point on the perpendicular axis.

$$I_Z = I_X + I_Y$$

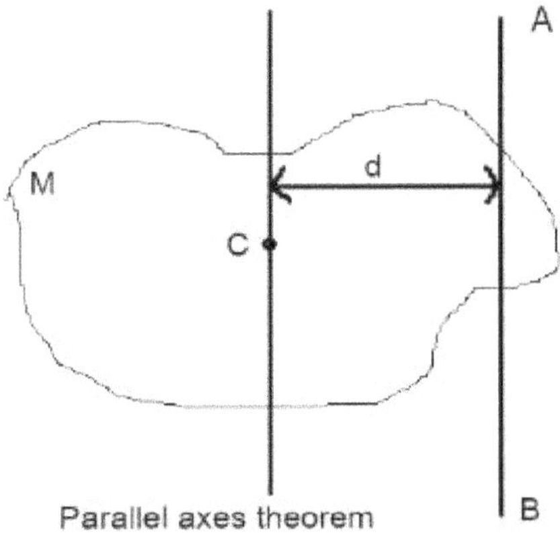

Figure IV.1: Parallel axes theorem

5 Marks Questions and Solutions

1. **a. State the Parallel Axes Theorem of Moment of Inertia.**
   b. Find the moment of inertia of a disc of mass 3kg and radius 50 cm about the following axes:

   - Axis passing through the center and perpendicular to the plane of the disc.

   - Axis touching the edge and perpendicular to the plane of the disc.

   - Axis passing through the center lying on the plane of the disc.

Solution:

a. The Parallel Axes Theorem states that the moment of inertia I_{AB} of an object about an axis parallel to an axis through its center of mass C is given by:

$$I_{AB} = I_C + Md^2$$

where:

- I_C is the moment of inertia about the center of mass,

- M is the mass of the object,

- d is the perpendicular distance between the two axes.

b. The moment of inertia of a disc with mass $M = 3\,\text{kg}$ and radius $R = 50\,\text{cm} = 0.5\,\text{m}$ about the following axes:

- Axis passing through the center and perpendicular to the plane of the disc:

$$I_{\text{center}} = \frac{1}{2}MR^2 = \frac{1}{2} \times 3 \times (0.5)^2 = 0.375\,\text{kg} \cdot \text{m}^2$$

- Axis touching the edge and perpendicular to the plane of the disc (using Parallel Axes Theorem):

$$I_{\text{edge}} = I_{\text{center}} + MR^2 = 0.375 + 3 \times (0.5)^2 = 1.125\,\text{kg} \cdot \text{m}^2$$

- Axis passing through the center lying on the plane of the disc:

$$I_{\text{plane}} = \frac{1}{4}MR^2 = \frac{1}{4} \times 3 \times (0.5)^2 = 0.1875\,\text{kg} \cdot \text{m}^2$$

2. **a. Define angular momentum.**
b. A thin ring of mass 5kg and diameter 20 cm is rotating about its axis passing through the center and perpendicular to the plane at 4200 rpm. Find its angular momentum.
Solution:

a. Angular momentum (L) is a vector quantity that describes the rotational motion of an object or system. It is the rotational equivalent of linear momentum. Angular momentum is given by:

$$L = r \times p = mr^2\omega$$

where m is the mass of the object, r is the perpendicular distance from the axis of rotation, and ω is the angular velocity.

b. For the thin ring:

- Mass $m = 5\,\text{kg}$,
- Diameter $d = 20\,\text{cm} = 0.2\,\text{m}$, so radius $r = 0.1\,\text{m}$,
- Angular velocity $\omega = 2\pi \times \nu = 2\pi \times 70\,\text{rpm} = 440\,\text{rad/s}$.

The moment of inertia of the ring about its axis is:

$$I = mr^2 = 5 \times (0.1)^2 = 0.05 \, \text{kg} \cdot \text{m}^2$$

Thus, the angular momentum is:

$$L = I\omega = 0.05 \times 440 = 22 \, \text{N} \cdot \text{m} \cdot \text{s}$$

3. **a. Define radius of gyration.**
   b. Derive an expression for the radius of gyration (K) for an 'n' particle system.
   c. The radius of gyration of a solid sphere of radius 'r' about a certain axis is 'r'. Find the distance of this axis from the center of the sphere.
   Solution:

a. The radius of gyration K is the distance from the axis of rotation at which the entire mass of a body can be considered to be concentrated without changing its moment of inertia. It is defined by the relation:

$$I = MK^2$$

where M is the mass of the object and I is its moment of inertia.

b. For an n-particle system, the moment of inertia about an axis of rotation is given by:

$$I = m_1 r_1^2 + m_2 r_2^2 + \cdots + m_n r_n^2$$

If K is the radius of gyration, then:

$$I = MK^2$$

where $M = m_1 + m_2 + \cdots + m_n$ is the total mass of the system. Thus, we can write:

$$MK^2 = \sum_{i=1}^{n} m_i r_i^2$$

This is the expression for the radius of gyration in terms of the individual masses and distances.

c. For a solid sphere, the moment of inertia about its diameter is:

$$I = \frac{2}{5}Mr^2$$

Let the distance of the new axis from the center of the sphere be x. By the Parallel Axes Theorem, the moment of inertia about the new axis is:

$$I = \frac{2}{5}Mr^2 + Mx^2$$

Since the radius of gyration about the new axis is r, we have:

$$I = Mr^2$$

Equating the two expressions for I, we get:

$$Mr^2 = \frac{2}{5}Mr^2 + Mx^2$$

Simplifying, we find:

$$x^2 = \frac{3}{5}r^2$$

Thus, the distance of the axis from the center of the sphere is:

$$x = \sqrt{\frac{3}{5}}r \approx 0.77r$$

4. **a. Define moment of inertia.**
   b. Two semi-circular discs of mass density 1 kg/m^2 and 2 kg/m^2, radius $r = 1$ m each are joined to form a complete disc. Find the moment of inertia of the complete disc about an axis passing through its center and perpendicular to the plane.
   Solution:

   a. The moment of inertia I is a measure of the rotational inertia of a body, i.e., the resistance to changes in its rotational motion. It is given by:

$$I = \sum m_i r_i^2$$

where m_i is the mass of a particle and r_i is the perpendicular distance of the particle from the axis of rotation.

b. Let the mass densities of the two semi-circular discs be $\sigma_1 = 1\,\text{kg/m}^2$ and $\sigma_2 = 2\,\text{kg/m}^2$, with radius $r = 1$ m. The area of each semi-circular disc is $A = \frac{1}{2}\pi r^2$. Hence, the masses of the two discs are:

$$m_1 = \sigma_1 A = 1 \times \frac{1}{2}\pi(1)^2 = \frac{\pi}{2}\,\text{kg}$$

$$m_2 = \sigma_2 A = 2 \times \frac{1}{2}\pi(1)^2 = \pi\,\text{kg}$$

The total mass of the complete disc is:

$$M = m_1 + m_2 = \frac{\pi}{2} + \pi = \frac{3\pi}{2}\,\text{kg}$$

The moment of inertia of the complete disc about an axis through its center and perpendicular to the plane is:

$$I = \frac{1}{2}Mr^2 = \frac{1}{2} \times \frac{3\pi}{2} \times (1)^2 = \frac{3\pi}{4}\,\text{kg}\cdot\text{m}^2$$

5. **Distinguish between Translational and Rotational Motion with examples.**
Solution:

Translational Motion:

- In translational motion, an object moves in a straight line or along a curved path without rotating.

- The motion is described by the displacement and direction of the object.

- Example: A car moving on a straight road or a ball falling vertically.

Rotational Motion:

- In rotational motion, an object spins or rotates around a central axis.

- The motion is described by the angle of rotation and the axis about which the object is rotating.

- Example: A wheel rotating around its axis, or a ceiling fan spinning around its central axis.

6. **If the Earth were to suddenly contract to half of its original size, by how much would the day be decreased? Given the moment of inertia of Earth is $I = 2MR^2$**
   Solution:

   Let the initial moment of inertia of Earth be:

   $$I_1 = 2MR^2$$

   where M is the mass of the Earth and R is the radius. After the Earth contracts to half of its original size, the new radius becomes $R/2$, and the new moment of inertia is:

   $$I_2 = 2M \left(\frac{R}{2}\right)^2 = \frac{1}{4}2MR^2$$

   According to the law of conservation of angular momentum:

   $$I_1\omega_1 = I_2\omega_2$$

   where ω_1 and ω_2 are the angular velocities before and after contraction. Since $\omega = \frac{2\pi}{T}$ (where T is the time period), we can write:

   $$\frac{2\pi}{T_1} = \frac{2\pi}{T_2} \times \frac{I_2}{I_1}$$

   Simplifying:

   $$T_2 = T_1 \times \frac{I_1}{I_2} = T_1 \times 4$$

   Since the original day length was 24 hours:

   $$T_2 = 24 \times \frac{1}{4} = 6\,\text{hours}$$

   Thus, the day would decrease by:

   $$24 - 6 = 18\,\text{hours}$$

7. **State and Explain the Law of Conservation of Angular Momentum.**
   Solution:

Statement: The angular momentum of a system remains constant if no external torque acts on it.

Explanation: The angular momentum L of a rotating body is given by:

$$L = I\omega$$

where I is the moment of inertia and ω is the angular velocity. If no external torque is acting on the body, then the angular momentum is conserved, which means:

$$\frac{dL}{dt} = \tau = 0$$

where τ is the external torque. Therefore, the angular momentum L remains constant over time:

$$L = \text{constant}$$

8. **Derive an expression showing the relationship between torque and moment of inertia, and hence define moment of inertia. Solution:**

Torque τ is defined as the force F applied at a distance r from the axis of rotation:

$$\tau = rF$$

For rotational motion, the force F can be related to mass and acceleration by $F = ma$, and the linear acceleration a is related to angular acceleration α by $a = r\alpha$. Thus, the torque becomes:

$$\tau = r \cdot mr\alpha = mr^2\alpha$$

But $I = mr^2$ is the moment of inertia of a body, so the torque can be written as:

$$\tau = I\alpha$$

This shows the relationship between torque and moment of inertia. The moment of inertia is defined as the resistance of an object to changes in its rotational motion and is given by:

$$I = \sum m_i r_i^2$$

where m_i is the mass of each particle and r_i is the distance from the axis of rotation.

9. **A force $\vec{F} = 2\hat{i} + 3\hat{j} - 2\hat{k}$ N acts on a particle at coordinates $(1, 2, -2)$ m. Find the torque on the particle.**

   Solution:

   The torque $\vec{\tau}$ is given by the cross product of the position vector $\vec{r}$ and the force vector $\vec{F}$:

   $$\vec{\tau} = \vec{r} \times \vec{F}$$

   Given:

   $$\vec{r} = 1\hat{i} + 2\hat{j} - 2\hat{k}, \quad \vec{F} = 2\hat{i} + 3\hat{j} - 2\hat{k}$$

   The cross product is calculated as:

   $$\vec{\tau} = \begin{vmatrix} \hat{i} & \hat{j} & \hat{k} \\ 1 & 2 & -2 \\ 2 & 3 & -2 \end{vmatrix}$$

   Expanding the determinant:

   $$\vec{\tau} = \hat{i}\,(2 \times (-2) - (-2) \times 3) - \hat{j}\,(1 \times (-2) - (-2) \times 2) \\ + \,\hat{k}\,(1 \times 3 - 2 \times 2) \tag{IV.1}$$

   $$\vec{\tau} = \hat{i}(-4 + 6) - \hat{j}(-2 + 4) + \hat{k}(3 - 4)$$

   $$\vec{\tau} = 2\hat{i} - 2\hat{j} - \hat{k}$$

   Thus, the torque is:

   $$\vec{\tau} = 2\hat{i} - 2\hat{j} - \hat{k}\,\text{N} \cdot \text{m}$$

   The magnitude of the torque is:

   $$|\vec{\tau}| = \sqrt{2^2 + (-2)^2 + (-1)^2} = \sqrt{9} = 3\,\text{N} \cdot \text{m}$$

10. **Find the moment of inertia of a disc:**

    (a) about its diameter

(b) about a tangent perpendicular to its plane.

Solution:

i. Moment of inertia about the diameter: Using the perpendicular axis theorem:

$$I_z = I_x + I_y$$

For a disc:

$$I_x = I_y = \frac{1}{4}MR^2$$

So:

$$I_z = \frac{1}{2}MR^2$$

ii. Moment of inertia about a tangent perpendicular to the plane: Using the parallel axis theorem:

$$I_t = I_c + MR^2$$

where $I_c = \frac{1}{2}MR^2$ is the moment of inertia about the center, and the distance from the center to the tangent is R. Therefore:

$$I_t = \frac{1}{2}MR^2 + MR^2 = \frac{3}{2}MR^2$$

11. **A particle of mass 3 kg is moving with a velocity of $\vec{v} = (3\hat{i} + 4\hat{j})$ m/s.**

   (a) Find the angular momentum of the particle about the origin when it is located at the point $\vec{r} = (2\hat{i} + 2\hat{j})$ m.

   (b) Calculate the magnitude of the angular momentum.

   (c) If the particle continues to move in a straight line, explain whether the angular momentum about the origin will remain constant or change over time, justifying your answer.

Ans:

   (a) The angular momentum $\vec{L}$ of a particle about a point (here, the origin) is given by:

$$\vec{L} = \vec{r} \times \vec{p}$$

where: - $\vec{r} = (2\hat{i} + 2\hat{j})$ m is the position vector of the particle, - $\vec{p} = m\vec{v}$ is the linear momentum of the particle, with $m = 3$ kg and $\vec{v} = (3\hat{i} + 4\hat{j})$ m/s.

First, calculate the linear momentum $\vec{p}$:

$$\vec{p} = m\vec{v} = 3 \times (3\hat{i} + 4\hat{j}) = (9\hat{i} + 12\hat{j}) \text{ kg m/s}$$

Now, calculate the cross product $\vec{L} = \vec{r} \times \vec{p}$:

$$\vec{L} = \begin{vmatrix} \hat{i} & \hat{j} & \hat{k} \\ 2 & 2 & 0 \\ 9 & 12 & 0 \end{vmatrix}$$

Expanding the determinant:

$$\vec{L} = \hat{i}(2 \cdot 0 - 0 \cdot 12) - \hat{j}(2 \cdot 0 - 0 \cdot 9) + \hat{k}(2 \cdot 12 - 2 \cdot 9)$$

$$\vec{L} = \hat{k}(24 - 18) = 6\hat{k} \text{ kg m}^2/\text{s}$$

(b) The magnitude of the angular momentum is:

$$|\vec{L}| = 6 \text{ kg m}^2/\text{s}$$

(c) Since there is no external torque acting on the particle about the origin (assuming it moves in a straight line with constant velocity), the angular momentum about the origin will remain constant. This is due to the principle of conservation of angular momentum, which states that in the absence of an external torque, the angular momentum of a system remains conserved.

Answer:

- (a) The angular momentum of the particle about the origin is $\vec{L} = 6\hat{k}$ kg m^2/s.

- (b) The magnitude of the angular momentum is 6 kg m^2/s.

- (c) The angular momentum about the origin remains constant as there is no external torque acting on the particle.

Chapter V

Unit V: Properties of Matter

2 Marks Questions and Solutions

1. **Define pressure with its SI unit.**

   Answer: Pressure at a point in a fluid is the average force acting per unit area surrounding that point. If the magnitude of average force exerted on the fluid is F and the area is A, then pressure is defined as:

   $$P = \frac{F}{A}$$

   The SI unit of pressure is Pascal (Pa), where:

   $$1\,\text{Pa} = 1\,\text{N/m}^2$$

2. **What is atmospheric pressure and 1 atm is equivalent to how much Pascal?**

   Answer: Atmospheric pressure is the force per unit area exerted by the air column on the Earth's surface. The standard value of atmospheric pressure is:

   $$1\,\text{atm} = 1.013 \times 10^5\,\text{Pa}$$

3. **Distinguish between absolute pressure and gauge pressure.**

   Answer:

   - **Absolute Pressure:** The pressure measured relative to a perfect vacuum. It is the sum of the atmospheric pressure and the pressure due to the liquid column in a tube. Mathematically:

   $$P_{\text{absolute}} = P_{\text{atm}} + \rho g h$$

   where ρ is the fluid density, g is the acceleration due to gravity, and h is the height of the liquid column.

- **Gauge Pressure:** The pressure measured relative to atmospheric pressure. It is given by:

$$P_{\text{gauge}} = P_{\text{absolute}} - P_{\text{atm}} = \rho g h$$

4. **Write the SI unit and dimensional formula of surface tension.**

   Answer: The SI unit of surface tension is Newton per meter (N/m), and the dimensional formula is:

$$[M^1 L^0 T^{-2}]$$

5. **Define cohesive force.**

   Answer: The force of attraction between the molecules of the same substance is called cohesive force.

6. **Define adhesive force.**

   Answer: The force of attraction between the molecules of different substances is called adhesive force.

7. **Define angle of contact.**

   Answer: The angle between the tangent at the solid surface and the tangent at the liquid surface at the contact point is called the angle of contact.

8. **State the effect of increase in temperature on surface tension.**

   Answer: The surface tension of a liquid decreases with a rise in temperature because the cohesive force between the molecules decreases as temperature increases.

9. **State Hooke's law and write the expression for it.**

   Answer: Hooke's Law states that, within the elastic limit, the stress in a body is directly proportional to the strain produced in it. The mathematical expression is:

$$\text{Stress} = E \cdot \text{Strain}$$

where E is the modulus of elasticity.

10. **What is the modulus of elasticity and write the types of moduli of elasticity?**

    Answer: The modulus of elasticity is the ratio of stress to strain. There are three types of moduli of elasticity:

    - Young's Modulus of Elasticity

    - Bulk Modulus

    - Shear Modulus

11. **State Stoke's law.**

    Answer: Stoke's law states that the viscous force F acting on a small sphere falling through a fluid is directly proportional to the radius r of the sphere, its velocity v through the fluid, and the coefficient of viscosity η of the fluid. The equation is:

    $$F = 6\pi\eta r v$$

    where η is the coefficient of viscosity, r is the radius of the sphere, and v is the velocity of the sphere.

12. **Give two industrial applications of viscosity.**
    Answer:

    - Viscosity determines the self-leveling and pumping behavior of paints, coatings, and adhesives.

    - Viscosity is considered when designing the flow and texture of cosmetic products such as creams and lotions.

13. **Define terminal velocity. Does terminal velocity exist in a vacuum?**
    Answer:

    - Terminal velocity is the highest velocity attained by an object falling through a fluid when the sum of the drag force and buoyant force is equal to the downward gravitational force.

    - In a vacuum, since there is no drag force, terminal velocity does not exist.

14. **In a steady, incompressible fluid flow through a conduit with varying cross-sectional area, how does the velocity of the fluid change as the area of the cross-section increases?**

    In a steady, incompressible fluid flow through a conduit with varying cross-sectional area, the velocity of the fluid changes according to the equation of continuity:

    $$A_1 V_1 = A_2 V_2$$

    where A_1 and A_2 are the cross-sectional areas at two points, and V_1 and V_2 are the corresponding velocities. If the cross-sectional area increases $(A_2 > A_1)$, the velocity decreases $(V_2 < V_1)$.

15. **Define the Reynolds number and explain its significance in determining the type of fluid flow.**

    Answer: The Reynolds number (Re) is defined as the ratio of inertial forces to viscous forces in a fluid and is given by:

    $$\mathrm{Re} = \frac{\rho v D}{\mu}$$

    where ρ is the fluid density, v is the velocity, D is the diameter of the pipe, and μ is the dynamic viscosity. The significance of Reynolds number in determining the type of flow is:

    - Laminar flow: $\mathrm{Re} < 2300$

    - Turbulent flow: $\mathrm{Re} > 4000$

    - Transient flow: $2300 < \mathrm{Re} < 4000$

16. **What is the difference between an elastic body and a plastic body?**
    Answer:

    - An elastic body regains its original shape and size after the removal of an external force (e.g., rubber bands).

    - A plastic body does not regain its original shape after the removal of an external force (e.g., clay or mud).

17. **Find:**

(i) The change in pressure, and

(ii) The final pressure

on an air-filled balloon from the following data: initial volume $V_i = 8 \times 10^{-3}$ m^3, initial pressure $P_i = 10^5$ N/m^2, decrease in volume $\Delta V = 10^{-3}$ m^3, and compressibility of air $k = 7.65 \times 10^{-6}$ m^2/N.

Solution:

Compressibility (k) is defined as the fractional change in volume per unit increase in pressure:

$$k = -\frac{1}{V_i}\frac{\Delta V}{\Delta P}$$

Rearranging for ΔP, the change in pressure, we get:

$$\Delta P = -\frac{\Delta V}{kV_i}$$

Substitute the given values:

$$\Delta P = -\frac{10^{-3}}{7.65 \times 10^{-6} \times 8 \times 10^{-3}}$$

Calculating this:

$$\Delta P \approx -1.63 \times 10^4 \, \text{N/m}^2$$

The negative sign indicates an increase in pressure. So, the increase in pressure is:

$$\Delta P = 1.63 \times 10^4 \, \text{N/m}^2$$

1. **Change in pressure:** $\Delta P = 1.63 \times 10^4 \, \text{N/m}^2$

2. **Final pressure:** Adding ΔP to the initial pressure P_i:

$$P_f = P_i + \Delta P = 10^5 + 1.63 \times 10^4 = 1.163 \times 10^5 \, \text{N/m}^2$$

Thus, the final pressure is:

$$P_f = 1.163 \times 10^5 \, \text{N/m}^2$$

5 Marks Questions & Solutions

1. **Write down the applications of surface tension.**
   Answer:

   - Surface tension is used in detergent formation to improve cleaning properties. Soap and detergent decrease the surface tension of water, making it easier for water to soak into pores and holes.

   - Surface tension is used for the characterization of food and packaging products.

   - Toothpaste on the brush spreads freely within the mouth and cleans the teeth more easily as it contains soap, which reduces the surface tension.

   - A small needle can float on the surface of water due to the surface tension of the water.

   - Kerosene oil in lanterns rises through the capillaries in the cotton wick and burns.

   - Surface tension is used in clinical tests for jaundice.

   - Antiseptics have low surface tension, which helps them spread faster on the skin.

2. **Write the construction and applications of Fortin's Barometer.**
   Answer:
   Construction: The Fortin's Barometer is used for accurate measurement of atmospheric pressure. It was designed by Nicolas Fortin in the late 18th century. The barometer consists of:

   - A vertical glass tube filled with mercury, enclosed in a brass casing.

   - The top part of the casing is transparent to allow viewing of the mercury level.

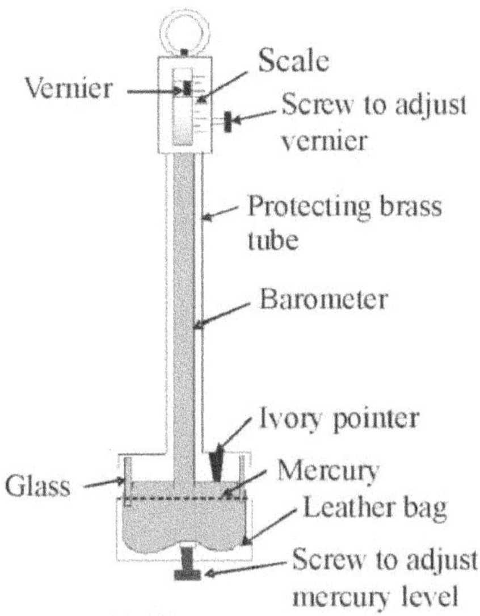

Figure V.1: Fortin's Barometer

- A millimetre-scale with a vernier scale is used to measure the height of the mercury column.

- The zero of the scale is at the tip of an ivory pointer fixed at the bottom of the brass tube.

- The mercury reservoir is a leather bag, which can be raised or lowered by a screw to adjust the mercury height.

The height of the mercury column is adjusted so that the tip of the pointer touches the mercury surface. The barometer measures the height of the mercury column, and the atmospheric pressure is determined using the formula:

$$P = \rho g h$$

where ρ is the density of mercury, g is the acceleration due to gravity, and h is the height of the mercury column.

Applications:

- It is commonly used to measure atmospheric pressure in meteorological stations, laboratories, and schools.

- It is used to measure the altitude of mountains and is important in weather forecasting.

3. **A steel rod with a length of 2 m and a cross-sectional area of 0.01 m² is subjected to a tensile force of 50,000 N. If the rod stretches by 2 mm, calculate the Young's modulus of the steel.**
Answer:

Given:

$$L = 2\,\text{m}, \quad A = 0.01\,\text{m}^2, \quad F = 50{,}000\,\text{N},$$
$$\Delta L = 2\,\text{mm} = 0.002\,\text{m} \tag{V.1}$$

Stress:

$$\sigma = \frac{F}{A} = \frac{50{,}000}{0.01} = 5{,}000{,}000\,\text{Pa}$$

Strain:

$$\epsilon = \frac{\Delta L}{L} = \frac{0.002}{2} = 0.001$$

Young's Modulus:

$$E = \frac{\sigma}{\epsilon} = \frac{5{,}000{,}000}{0.001} = 5 \times 10^9\,\text{Pa}$$

Thus, the Young's modulus of the steel is 5×10^9 Pa.

4. **State Stoke's law. Obtain expression for viscous force from Stoke's law using dimensional analysis.**
Answer:

Stoke's Law: Stoke's law states that the viscous force F acting on a small sphere falling through a fluid is directly proportional to the radius r of the sphere, its velocity v through the fluid, and the coefficient of viscosity η of the fluid. The equation is given by:

$$F \propto r^a v^b \eta^c$$

or,

$$F = k r^a v^b \eta^c$$

where k is a dimensionless constant.

Dimensional Analysis: The dimensions of force F are $[M^1 L^1 T^{-2}]$. The dimensions of radius r are $[L^1]$, the dimensions of velocity v are $[L^1 T^{-1}]$, and the dimensions of coefficient of viscosity η are $[M^1 L^{-1} T^{-1}]$.

Now, equating the dimensions on both sides of the equation $F = k r^a v^b \eta^c$:

$$[M^1 L^1 T^{-2}] = [L^a][L^b T^{-b}][M^c L^{-c} T^{-c}]$$

Simplifying:

$$[M^1 L^1 T^{-2}] = [M^c L^{a+b-c} T^{-b-c}]$$

By comparing the powers of M, L, and T, we get:

$$c = 1, \quad a + b - c = 1, \quad -b - c = -2$$

From the third equation $-b - c = -2$, we get $b = 1$, and substituting into $a + b - c = 1$, we get $a = 1$.

Thus, the equation becomes:

$$F = k r v \eta$$

From experimental determination, $k = 6\pi$, so the final expression for the viscous force is:

$$F = 6\pi r v \eta$$

5. **Write five applications of Bernoulli's Theorem.**
   Answer:

   - Bernoulli's theorem is used in the Venturimeter (or flowmeter) to measure the flow rate of fluids through pipes.

   - It is used in the design of carburetors in automobiles, as well as in filter pumps, atomizers, and sprayers.

   - The Magnus effect, which is explained by Bernoulli's principle, plays an important role in sports like golf, cricket, soccer, and tennis, where spinning balls curve in the air.

- Bernoulli's principle explains the phenomenon of roofs being blown off during hurricanes and tornados, and why nearby rowboats move towards each other when moving in parallel.

- Bernoulli's theorem also explains the phenomenon of blood flow in vessels and the occurrence of heart attacks due to atherosclerosis.

6. **Consider that water is flowing in a fire hose with a velocity of 2.0 m/s and pressure of 250,000 Pa. The pressure decreases to atmospheric pressure (101,300 Pa) at the nozzle. Assume that there is no change in height. Calculate the velocity of the water leaving the nozzle. The density of water is 1000 kgm^{-3}. Gravitational acceleration $g = 9.8$ m/s^2.**

Answer: According to Bernoulli's principle,

$$P_1 + \rho g h_1 + \frac{1}{2}\rho V_1^2 = P_2 + \rho g h_2 + \frac{1}{2}\rho V_2^2$$

Since $h_1 = h_2$, we can rewrite this equation as:

$$P_1 + \frac{1}{2}\rho V_1^2 = P_2 + \frac{1}{2}\rho V_2^2$$

Solving for V_2:

$$V_2 = \sqrt{\frac{2}{\rho}\left(\frac{1}{2}\rho V_1^2 + P_1 - P_2\right)}$$

Substitute the known values:

$$V_2 = \sqrt{\frac{2}{1000}\left(\frac{1}{2} \times 1000 \times 2^2 + 250,000 - 101,300\right)}$$

$$V_2 = \sqrt{301.4} = 17.36 \text{ m/s}$$

7. **Write down the applications of Surface Tension.**

   Answer: Surface Tension has many applications in our daily life, such as:

   (i) Surface tension is used in detergent formation to improve cleaning properties. Soap and detergent decrease the surface tension of water so that water soaks into pores and holes easily.

   (ii) Surface tension is used for the characterization of food and packing products.

   (iii) Toothpaste on the brush spreads freely within the mouth and cleans the teeth more easily as it contains soap, which reduces the surface tension.

   (iv) A small needle can float on the water surface because of the surface tension of water.

   (v) The kerosene oil in lanterns rises through the capillaries in the cotton wick and burns.

   (vi) Surface tension is used in clinical tests for jaundice.

   (vii) Antiseptics like Dettol have low surface tension, which helps them spread faster.

Chapter VI

Unit VI: Heat and Thermometry

2 Marks Questions & Solutions

Q.1 - Explain the difference between heat and temperature.

Ans.:

Heat is a form of energy that is associated with the overall kinetic energy of the molecules of a substance. It flows from a region of higher temperature to a region of lower temperature. Heat is measured in Joules (J) or calories.

Temperature, on the other hand, is a measure of the average kinetic energy of the molecules of a substance. It indicates the degree of hotness or coldness of an object. Temperature is measured in Kelvin (K) in the SI system, as well as in Celsius ($^\circ C$) and Fahrenheit ($^\circ F$).

Q.2 - Name the general mode of heat transfer in solids, liquids, and gases.

Ans.:

(a) The general mode of heat transfer in solids is *conduction*.

(b) The general mode of heat transfer in liquids and gases is *convection*.

Q.3 - Define Radiation. Give an example.

Ans.:

Radiation is the method of transferring heat from one body to another without the involvement of any medium in between. It does not require a material medium to propagate, unlike conduction and convection. An example of radiation is the heat from the Sun reaching the Earth through the vacuum of space.

Q.4 - Define Coefficient of Thermal Conductivity and write its dimensional formula.

Ans.:

The coefficient of thermal conductivity (denoted by K) of a substance is defined as the amount of heat passing through a unit area of the material per unit time per unit temperature gradient. Mathematically,

$$K = \frac{Q \cdot l}{A \cdot \Delta T}$$

where Q is the heat transferred, l is the length of the material, A is the cross-sectional area, and ΔT is the temperature difference.

The dimensional formula of the coefficient of thermal conductivity is:

$$[K] = [M^1 L^1 T^{-3} \theta^{-1}]$$

where θ represents the temperature unit.

Q.5 - What is the Coefficient of Superficial Expansion of a solid?

Ans.:

The Coefficient of Superficial Expansion (β) of a solid is defined as the increase in area per unit area at $0°C$ for a unit rise in temperature. Mathematically,

$$\beta = \frac{A_t - A_0}{A_0 t}$$

where A_t is the area of the solid at temperature t, and A_0 is the area of the solid at $0°C$.

Q.6 - Define the Coefficient of Linear Expansion of a solid.

Ans.:

The Coefficient of Linear Expansion (α) of a solid is defined as the increase in length per unit length at $0°C$ for a unit rise in temperature. Mathematically,

$$\alpha = \frac{l_t - l_0}{l_0 t}$$

where l_t is the length of the solid at temperature t, and l_0 is the length of the solid at $0°C$.

Q.7 - Define the Coefficient of Cubical Expansion of a solid.

Ans.:

The Coefficient of Cubical Expansion (γ) of a solid is defined as the increase in volume per unit volume at $0°C$ for a unit rise in temperature. Mathematically,

$$\gamma = \frac{V_t - V_0}{V_0 t}$$

where V_t is the volume of the solid at temperature t, and V_0 is the volume of the solid at $0°C$.

Q.8 - Define Mercury Thermometer and write its two uses.

Ans.:

A mercury thermometer is a temperature-measuring device that uses mercury, a liquid metal, contained in a glass tube. As the temperature rises, the mercury expands and rises in the tube, providing a visual indication of temperature on a calibrated scale.

Uses:

1. *Medical Use:* For measuring body temperature.

2. *Laboratory Use:* For measuring temperatures during chemical reactions or experiments.

Q.9 - Define Bimetallic Thermometer and write its two applications.

Ans.:

A bimetallic thermometer consists of two different metals bonded together in a strip or coil. When the temperature changes, the differing rates of expansion of the two metals cause the strip or coil to bend. This movement is then translated into a temperature reading on a calibrated scale.

Applications:

1. *Industrial Use:* Commonly used in industries to measure the temperature of gases, liquids, and solids.

2. *Home Appliances:* Used in cooking appliances like ovens and refrigerators.

Q.10 - Define Platinum Thermometer and write its two uses.

Ans.:

A platinum thermometer is a highly precise temperature measuring device that utilizes the resistance of platinum wire to determine temperature. As the temperature changes, the electrical resistance of the platinum wire changes in a predictable manner, allowing for accurate temperature readings.

Uses:

1. *Research and Development:* Used in scientific research for precise temperature measurements.

2. *Low-Temperature Measurements:* Used in cryogenic applications to measure extremely low temperatures.

Q.11 - Define Specific Heat Capacity and mention its SI unit.

Ans.:

Specific heat capacity is the amount of heat required to raise the temperature of 1 kilogram of a substance by 1 Kelvin. The SI unit of specific heat capacity is Joules per kilogram per Kelvin (J/kg·K).

Q.12 - Explain the difference between Specific Heat at Constant Pressure (C_p) and Specific Heat at Constant Volume (C_v).

Ans.:

C_p: Specific heat at constant pressure is the amount of heat required to raise the temperature of a unit mass by one unit degree while keeping the pressure constant.

C_v: Specific heat at constant volume is the amount of heat required to raise the temperature of a unit mass by one unit degree while keeping the volume constant.

Q.13 - Write the relations between specific heats C_p and C_v.

Ans.:

The following relations hold between C_p and C_v: 1. $\frac{C_p}{C_v} = \gamma$, where γ is the adiabatic index or isentropic expansion factor. 2. $C_p - C_v = R$, where R is the universal gas constant.

Q.14 - Convert 77°F to Celsius.

Ans.:

To convert Fahrenheit to Celsius:

$$T_C = \frac{5}{9}(T_F - 32)$$

Substitute $T_F = 77°F$:

$$T_C = \frac{5}{9}(77 - 32) = 25°C$$

Q.15 - Convert 25°C to Fahrenheit.

Ans.:

To convert Celsius to Fahrenheit:

$$T_F = \frac{9}{5}T_C + 32$$

Substitute $T_C = 25°C$:

$$T_F = \frac{9}{5}(25) + 32 = 77°F$$

Q.16 - Convert 25°C to Kelvin.

Ans.:

To convert Celsius to Kelvin:

$$T_K = T_C + 273.15$$

Substitute $T_C = 25°C$:

$$T_K = 25 + 273.15 = 298.15\,K$$

Q.17 State the effect of increase in temperature on surface tension.

Ans.:

The surface tension of a liquid decreases with rise in temperature because the cohesive force decreases due to an increase in its temperature. **Q18: Good bricks are the ones that have low thermal conductivity to keep the house cool in summer and warm in winter. Red bricks have thermal conductivity 0.6 W/m·K. If the temperature at one end of such a brick** is 45°C and at the other end it is 26°C, and the separation distance between the two ends is 10 cm, find the time rate of heat flux passing through the brick.

Ans: We can use Fourier's law of heat conduction to calculate the rate of heat flux through the brick:

$$Q = \frac{kA(T_1 - T_2)}{L}$$

Where: - Q is the rate of heat transfer (W), - k is the thermal conductivity (0.6 W/m·K), - A is the cross-sectional area (m^2), - T_1 and T_2 are the temperatures at the two ends (45°C and 26°C), - L is the separation distance (10 cm = 0.1 m).

Assuming a unit cross-sectional area, $A = 1\ \text{m}^2$, the rate of heat transfer is:

$$Q = \frac{0.6 \times 1 \times (45 - 26)}{0.1} = \frac{0.6 \times 19}{0.1} = 114\,\text{W}$$

Thus, the time rate of heat flux passing through the brick is 114 W.

5 Marks Questions & Solutions

Q1 - Derive the relation between the coefficient of linear expansion and the coefficient of superficial expansion.

Ans.:

Consider a thin square metal plate. Let l_0 be the length of the side of the square and A_0 be the area of the square at temperature $0°C$. Upon heating, the square expands and let l_t be the length of the side of the square and A_t be the area of the square at temperature $t°C$.

The area of the square at $0°C$ is:

$$A_0 = l_0^2$$

The area of the square at $t°C$ is:

$$A_t = l_t^2$$

The coefficient of linear expansion α is defined as:

$$\alpha = \frac{l_t - l_0}{l_0 t}$$

or

$$l_t - l_0 = \alpha l_0 t$$

which gives

$$l_t = l_0(\alpha t + 1)$$

Now, using the definition of the coefficient of superficial expansion β, we have:

$$\beta = \frac{A_t - A_0}{A_0 t}$$

Substitute $A_t = l_t^2$ and $A_0 = l_0^2$:

$$\beta = \frac{l_t^2 - l_0^2}{l_0^2 t}$$

Substitute $l_t = l_0(\alpha t + 1)$ from equation (3):

$$\beta = \frac{[l_0(\alpha t + 1)]^2 - l_0^2}{l_0^2 t}$$

Simplify the expression:

$$\beta = \frac{l_0^2 \left[(\alpha t + 1)^2 - 1\right]}{l_0^2 t}$$

$$\beta = \frac{\left[(\alpha t + 1)^2 - 1\right]}{t}$$

$$\beta = \frac{(\alpha^2 t^2 + 2\alpha t + 1 - 1)}{t}$$

$$\beta = \frac{\alpha^2 t^2 + 2\alpha t}{t}$$

$$\beta = \alpha^2 t + 2\alpha$$

Since α is very small for solids, $\alpha^2 t$ can be neglected. Therefore, we have:

$$\beta \approx 2\alpha$$

Q2 - Derive the relation between the coefficient of linear expansion and the coefficient of cubical expansion.

Ans.:

Consider a metallic cube. Let l_0 be the length of the side of the cube and V_0 be the volume of the cube at temperature $0°C$. Upon heating, the cube expands and let l_t be the length of the side of the cube and V_t be the volume of the cube at temperature $t°C$.

The volume of the cube at $0°C$ is:

$$V_0 = l_0^3$$

The volume of the cube at $t°C$ is:

$$V_t = l_t^3$$

The coefficient of linear expansion α is given by:

$$\alpha = \frac{l_t - l_0}{l_0 t}$$

or

$$l_t - l_0 = \alpha l_0 t$$

which gives

$$l_t = l_0(\alpha t + 1)$$

Now, using the definition of the coefficient of cubical expansion γ, we have:

$$\gamma = \frac{V_t - V_0}{V_0 t}$$

Substitute $V_t = l_t^3$ and $V_0 = l_0^3$:

$$\gamma = \frac{l_t^3 - l_0^3}{l_0^3 t}$$

Substitute $l_t = l_0(\alpha t + 1)$ from equation (3):

$$\gamma = \frac{[l_0(\alpha t + 1)]^3 - l_0^3}{l_0^3 t}$$

Simplify the expression:

$$\gamma = \frac{l_0^3 \left[(\alpha t + 1)^3 - 1\right]}{l_0^3 t}$$

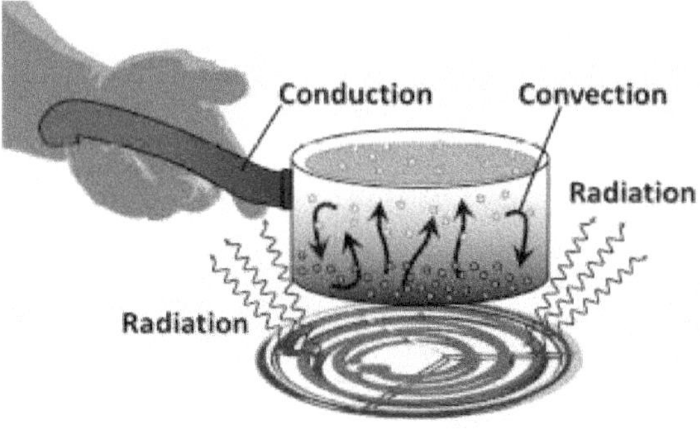

Figure VI.1: Mode of heat transfer

$$\gamma = \frac{\left[(\alpha t + 1)^3 - 1\right]}{t}$$

$$\gamma = \frac{\alpha^3 t^3 + 3\alpha^2 t^2 + 3\alpha t + 1 - 1}{t}$$

$$\gamma = \frac{\alpha^3 t^3 + 3\alpha^2 t^2 + 3\alpha t}{t}$$

$$\gamma = \alpha^3 t^2 + 3\alpha^2 t + 3\alpha$$

Since α is very small for solids, we can neglect $\alpha^3 t^2$ and $3\alpha^2 t$, so we are left with:

$$\gamma \approx 3\alpha$$

Q3 - Explain various modes of heat transfer with examples.

Ans.:

There are three primary modes of heat transfer: Conduction, Convection, and Radiation.

1. Conduction:

In solids, heat transfers via the molecular vibrations of molecules that are in direct contact with each other. In this case, heat is transferred without the actual movement of particles. The heat energy is passed from the hotter part of the material to the cooler part through collisions between adjacent molecules. An example of conduction is the heating of one end of a metal rod, where the heat gradually spreads to the cooler end.

2. Convection:

In fluids (liquids or gases), the transfer of heat takes place due to the actual movement of particles from one place to another. As the fluid gets heated, its particles gain kinetic energy, expand, and move upwards. Cooler, denser fluid then takes its place, forming convection currents. An example of convection is the heating of water in a pot, where the hot water rises while the cooler water sinks, creating circulating currents.

3. Radiation:

Radiation is the transfer of heat through electromagnetic waves, and it does not require a medium. Heat energy is radiated in the form of infrared rays. An example of radiation is the heat felt from the Sun, which reaches Earth through the vacuum of space. Another example is the heat emitted by a fire, which can be felt even without direct contact with the flames.

Q4 - A scientist measures the temperature of a gas as 315 K. Using this information:

(i) Convert the temperature to Celsius and Fahrenheit.

(ii) If the gas is cooled down to 77°F, what will be its temperature in Kelvin and Celsius?

Ans.:

(i) To convert the temperature from Kelvin to Celsius:

$$T_C = T_K - 273.15 = 315 - 273.15 = 41.85°C$$

To convert Celsius to Fahrenheit:

$$T_F = \frac{9}{5}T_C + 32 = \frac{9}{5} \times 41.85 + 32 = 107.33°F$$

(ii) To convert 77°F to Celsius:

$$T_C = \frac{5}{9}(T_F - 32) = \frac{5}{9}(77 - 32) = 25°C$$

To convert Celsius to Kelvin:

$$T_K = T_C + 273.15 = 25 + 273.15 = 298.15K$$

Q5 - Derive the expression for the coefficient of thermal conductivity (K). Write its SI unit and dimensional formula.

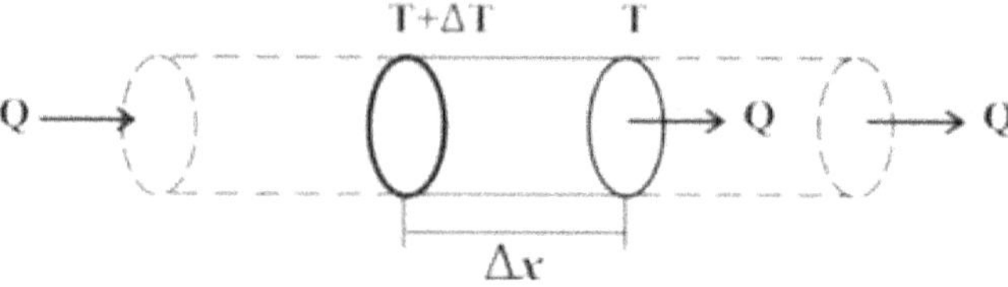

Figure VI.2: Conduction of heat :Q.5

Ans.:

Let us consider a bar of material with cross-sectional area A and length Δx. The two isothermal surfaces of the bar are at temperatures T and $T + \Delta T$, where $T + \Delta T > T$, and heat flows from the surface at $T + \Delta T$ to the surface at T.

The quantity of heat conducted is directly proportional to:

1. The area of the cross-section: $Q \propto A$
2. The temperature gradient in the direction of heat flow: $Q \propto \frac{\Delta T}{\Delta x}$
3. The time for which the heat flows: $Q \propto t$

Thus, the quantity of heat conducted, Q, can be expressed as:

$$Q = -K \cdot A \cdot \frac{\Delta T}{\Delta x} \cdot t$$

This is Fourier's law of heat conduction. Here, K is the coefficient of thermal conductivity.

The SI unit of K is:

$$\text{SI unit of } K = \frac{\text{J}}{\text{m} \cdot \text{s} \cdot \text{K}} = \text{W/m} \cdot \text{K}$$

The dimensional formula of K is:

$$[K] = [M^1 L^1 T^{-3} \theta^{-1}]$$

Q6: Differentiate between thermal conductors and thermal insulators.

Ans:

- **Thermal Conductors:**

– Materials that allow heat to flow through them easily.

– Have high thermal conductivity, enabling efficient heat transfer.

– Examples: metals such as copper, aluminum, and iron.

– Used in applications requiring heat transfer, e.g., cooking utensils, heat exchangers.

• **Thermal Insulators:**

– Materials that resist the flow of heat.

– Have low thermal conductivity, preventing effective heat transfer.

– Examples: rubber, wood, glass wool, foam.

– Used to reduce heat loss or gain, e.g., in house insulation, refrigerators, thermoses.

Q 7: Explain the mode of heat transfer in liquid metal.

Ans:

Heat transfer in liquid metals occurs primarily through three modes: conduction, convection, and radiation.

– **Conduction:**

* In liquid metals, conduction occurs due to the movement of free electrons that carry thermal energy. Metals have high thermal conductivity, so they can quickly transfer heat from the hot region to the cooler regions within the liquid.

– **Convection:**

* Convection is the process by which heat is transferred by the bulk motion of the fluid. In liquid metals, this is facilitated by the movement of the metal itself, which can create temperature gradients. As the hotter portions of the liquid rise, the cooler portions sink, thus transferring heat.

– **Radiation:**

* Like any other material, liquid metals can transfer heat through radiation. The intensity of the radiative heat transfer depends on the temperature of the metal and the emissivity of the surface.

In practical applications, such as in nuclear reactors or metal casting processes, heat transfer in liquid metals is primarily governed by a combination of conduction and convection due to the high thermal conductivity of metals and their fluid nature.

Chapter VII

Important Formulae: Physical World, Units and Measurements

1. Formula for conversion of value of a given physical quantity from one system of units to another:

$$n_1 u_1 = n_2 u_2$$

where n_1 is the numerical value in the first system of units, u_1 is the unit of the physical quantity in the first system of units, n_2 is the numerical value in the second system of units, and u_2 is the unit of the physical quantity in the second system of units.

2. The least count (L.C) of Vernier Calipers is given by:

$$\text{Least Count} = \frac{\text{smallest division on main scale}}{\text{Total number of divisions on Vernier scale}} = \frac{\text{SDMS}}{\text{TDVS}}$$

$$= \frac{1\,\text{MSD}}{n}$$

3. Least count of micrometer screw gauge:

$$\text{Least Count} = \frac{\text{Pitch of screw gauge}}{\text{Number of divisions on circular scale}}$$

4. Least count of spherometer:

$$\text{Least Count} = \frac{\text{Pitch of the spherometer screw}}{\text{Number of divisions on circular scale}}$$

5. If values obtained are $a_1, a_2, a_3, \ldots, a_n$, then the arithmetic mean of these values is:

$$\bar{a} = a_{\text{mean}} = \frac{a_1 + a_2 + a_3 + \cdots + a_n}{n}$$

6. Errors in individual measurements can be written as:

$$\Delta a_1 = \bar{a} - a_1, \quad \Delta a_2 = \bar{a} - a_2, \quad \Delta a_3 = \bar{a} - a_3, \ldots$$

$$\Delta a_n = \bar{a} - a_n$$

7. Mean Absolute Error $(\overline{\Delta a})$:

$$\overline{|\Delta a|} = \frac{|\Delta a_1| + |\Delta a_2| + |\Delta a_3| + \cdots + |\Delta a_n|}{n}$$

8. Relative error (δa):

$$\delta a = \frac{\overline{|\Delta a|}}{\overline{a}}$$

9. Percentage error:

$$\delta a = \frac{\overline{|\Delta a|}}{\overline{a}} \times 100\%$$

10. Errors in a summation $(Z = X + Y)$ or a subtraction $(Z = X - Y)$:

$$\Delta Z = \Delta X + \Delta Y$$

11. Errors in a multiplication $(Z = XY)$ and a division $(Z = X/Y)$:

$$\frac{\Delta Z}{Z} = \frac{\Delta X}{X} + \frac{\Delta Y}{Y}$$

12. Error in a quantity with powers:

$$Z = k\frac{X^n Y^m}{C^q} \Rightarrow \frac{\Delta Z}{Z} = n\frac{\Delta X}{X} + m\frac{\Delta Y}{Y} + q\frac{\Delta C}{C}$$

Chapter VIII

Important Formulae :Force and Motion

Unit 2: Force and Motion

1. The unit vector of vector $\vec{A}$ is denoted as

$$\hat{A} = \frac{\vec{A}}{|\vec{A}|} = \frac{\text{vector}}{\text{magnitude of vector}}$$

2. The magnitude of $(\vec{a} + \vec{b})$ is given as

$$|\vec{a} + \vec{b}| = \sqrt{a^2 + b^2 + 2ab\cos\theta}$$

where θ is the angle between vectors $\vec{a}$ and $\vec{b}$.

3. If $(\vec{a} + \vec{b})$ makes an angle α with vector $\vec{a}$, then

$$\tan\alpha = \frac{b\sin\theta}{a + b\cos\theta}$$

4. If vector $\vec{A}$ makes an angle α with the X-axis and $\beta = (90° - \alpha)$ with the Y-axis, then the rectangular components along the X-axis and Y-axis are:

$$A_x = A\cos\alpha \quad \text{and} \quad A_y = A\cos\beta$$

Therefore, the vector $\vec{A}$ can be written as:

$$\vec{A} = A_x\vec{i} + A_y\vec{j} = (A\cos\alpha)\vec{i} + (A\cos\beta)\vec{j}$$

5. If the components A_x and A_y are given, then the magnitude of the vector $\vec{A}$ is

$$|\vec{A}| = \sqrt{A_x^2 + A_y^2} \quad \text{and} \quad \tan\alpha = \frac{A_y}{A_x}$$

6. Let $\vec{A} = A_x\vec{i} + A_y\vec{j} + A_z\vec{k}$ and $\vec{B} = B_x\vec{i} + B_y\vec{j} + B_z\vec{k}$.

$$\vec{A} \pm \vec{B} = (A_x \pm B_x)\vec{i} + (A_y \pm B_y)\vec{j} + (A_z \pm B_z)\vec{k}$$

The magnitude is:

$$|\vec{A} \pm \vec{B}| = \sqrt{(A_x \pm B_x)^2 + (A_y \pm B_y)^2 + (A_z \pm B_z)^2}$$

7. The dot product of two vectors $\vec{A}$ and $\vec{B}$ is given by:

$$\vec{A} \cdot \vec{B} = AB\cos\theta = |\vec{A}||\vec{B}|\cos\theta$$

where θ is the angle between vectors $\vec{A}$ and $\vec{B}$.

$$\vec{A} \cdot \vec{B} = A_x B_x + A_y B_y + A_z B_z$$

8. The cross product of two vectors $\vec{A}$ and $\vec{B}$, denoted by $\vec{A} \times \vec{B}$, is also a vector. Its magnitude is given by:

$$|\vec{A} \times \vec{B}| = AB\sin\theta$$

and its components are:

$$\vec{A} \times \vec{B} = (A_y B_z - A_z B_y)\vec{i} + (A_z B_x - A_x B_z)\vec{j} + (A_x B_y - A_y B_x)\vec{k}$$

9. The external applied force is

$$\vec{F} = k\frac{m(\vec{v}_2 - \vec{v}_1)}{\Delta t} \quad \text{or} \quad \vec{F} = ma$$

10. The thrust of a rocket is given by:

$$\text{Thrust} = \text{mass} \times \text{acceleration of rocket}$$

$$= \text{velocity of gases} \times \text{rate of mass decrease}$$

$$\vec{F} = m\frac{\Delta\vec{v}}{\Delta t} = \frac{\Delta m}{\Delta t}\vec{u}$$

11. Impulse is defined as:

$$\vec{I} = \vec{F}\Delta t = \vec{p}_2 - \vec{p}_1$$

12. Instantaneous angular velocity:

$$\omega = \lim_{\Delta t \to 0} \frac{\Delta \theta}{\Delta t} = \frac{d\theta}{dt}$$

13. Instantaneous angular acceleration:

$$\alpha = \lim_{\Delta t \to 0} \frac{\Delta \omega}{\Delta t} = \frac{d\omega}{dt}$$

14. Relation between linear velocity and angular velocity:

$$v = r\omega$$

15. Relation between linear acceleration and angular acceleration:

$$a = r\alpha$$

16. The equations for constant angular acceleration are:

$$\omega = \omega_0 + \alpha t \tag{VIII.1}$$

$$\theta = \omega_0 t + \frac{1}{2}\alpha t^2 \tag{VIII.2}$$

$$\omega^2 = \omega_0^2 + 2\alpha\theta \tag{VIII.3}$$

17. Centripetal force F_c = mass $\times$ centripetal acceleration = mv^2/r = $m\omega^2 r$

18. Velocity of vehicle on banked road $v = \sqrt{rg\tan\theta}$

Chapter IX

Important Formulae : Work, Power and Energy

1. Work $(W) = \mathbf{F} \bullet \mathbf{r} = F \cos\theta.r$, The work done by a variable force is given by:

$$W = \int \mathbf{F} \cdot d\mathbf{r}$$

2. Limiting Friction $= \mu_{\text{limiling}} \times ($ Normal Force (or normal reaction force$) = \mu_{\text{limiting}} N$

3. Limiting static friction, $f_s = \mu_s N = \mu_s mg$ and kinetic friction force $f_k = \mu_k N$

4. On inclined plane $\mu_k = \mu_s = \tan\theta$

5. kinetic energy $(KE) = \frac{1}{2}mv^2$ and gravitational potential energy $U = mgh$

6. Power $P = \frac{dW}{dt} = \frac{F \cdot dr}{dt} = F \cdot v \quad (W = F \cdot r \text{ and } \frac{dr}{dt} = v)$

Chapter X

Important Formulae : Rotational Motion

1. Torque $\vec{\tau} = \vec{r} \times \vec{F} = rF\sin\theta$

2. Angular momentum $\vec{L} = \vec{r} \times \vec{p} - mvr\sin\theta$

3. Moment of inertia $I = m_1 r_1{}^2 + m_2 r_2^2 + \cdots - \cdots + m_{II}r_n{}^2 = \sum_{i=1}^{n} m_i r_i{}^2$

4. Relation between torque and moment of inertia $\tau_{net} = \sum_{i=1}^{n} m_i r_i^2 \alpha = I\alpha$

5. Relation between angular momentum and moment of inertia $I_{net} = \sum_{i=1}^{n} m_i r_i^2 \omega = I\omega$

6. Radius of gyration $K = \sqrt{\dfrac{\sum_{i=1}^{n} m_i r_i^2}{M}}$ where moment of inertia of body $IM \times K^2$

7. Perpendicular axes theorem $I_z = I_x + I_y$

8. Parallel axes theorem $I_{AB} = I_C + Md^2$

9. When torque $= 0$ then $I_1\omega_1 = I_2\omega_2$ where $\dfrac{d\vec{L}}{dt} = \vec{\tau}_{net}$

10. M.I. of rod about an axis of rotation passes through the Centre and perpendicular to the length $I = \dfrac{Ml^2}{12}$

11. M.I. of disc about axis $= \frac{1}{2}Mr^2$, about diameter $= \frac{1}{4}Mr^2$, about tangent to rim, parallel to axis $= \frac{3}{2}Mr^2$, about tangent to rim, parallel to diameter $= \frac{5}{4}Mr^2$

12. M.I. of ring about axis $I = Mr^2$, about diameter $I = \frac{1}{2}Mr^2$, about tangent to rim, parallel to axis $= 2Mr^2$, about tangent to rim, parallel to diameter $= \frac{3}{2}Mr^2$

13. Moment of Inertia (M.I.) of a solid sphere about its diameter:

$$I = \frac{2}{5} M r^2$$

and about a tangent:

$$I = \frac{7}{5} M r^2$$

14. M.I. of a hollow sphere about its diameter:

$$I = \frac{2}{5} M \frac{r_2^5 - r_1^5}{r_2^3 - r_1^3}$$

15. M.I. of a spherical shell about its diameter:

$$I = \frac{2}{3} M r^2$$

Chapter XI

Important Formulae : Properties of Matter

1. Young's modulus:

$$Y = \frac{\text{Longitudinal stress}}{\text{Longitudinal strain}} = \frac{F/A}{\Delta L/L} = \frac{FL}{A\Delta L}$$

2. Bulk modulus:

$$B = \frac{\text{Volumetric stress}}{\text{Volumetric strain}} = \frac{\Delta P}{-\Delta V/V} = \frac{-V\Delta P}{\Delta V}$$

Compressibility:

$$K = \frac{1}{B}$$

3. Modulus of rigidity:

$$\eta = \frac{\text{Shear stress}}{\text{Shear strain}} = \frac{F/A}{x/L} = \frac{FL}{Ax}$$

4. Pressure:

$$P = \frac{F}{A}$$

Absolute pressure:

$$P = P_{\text{atm}} + \rho g h$$

Gauge pressure:

$$\text{Gauge pressure} = P - P_{\text{atm}} = \rho g h$$

5. Surface tension:

$$S = \frac{F}{l}$$

Ascent formula in capillary:

$$h = \frac{2s\cos\theta}{r\rho g}$$

6. Viscous force:

$$F = \eta A \frac{v_2 - v_1}{d}$$

where $\frac{v_2 - v_1}{d}$ is the velocity gradient.

7. Relation between kinematic viscosity and dynamic viscosity:

$$\nu = \frac{\eta}{\rho}$$

8. Terminal velocity:

$$V_t = \frac{2}{9} \frac{r^2 g}{\eta} (\rho - \rho_f)$$

9. Stokes' law:

$$F_V = 6\pi\eta r V$$

10. Temperature dependence of viscosity in liquids:

$$\eta = \frac{\eta_0}{1 + \alpha t + \beta t^2}$$

11. Temperature dependence of viscosity in gases:

$$\eta = \eta_0 + \alpha T + \beta T^2$$

12. Reynolds number:

$$R_e = \frac{\rho V D}{\eta} = \frac{V D}{\nu}$$

13. Continuity equation:

$$A_1 V_1 = A_2 V_2$$

or $AV = \text{constant} = Q$, where Q is the volume flow rate.

14. Bernoulli's equation:

$$P + \rho g h + \frac{1}{2}\rho V^2 = \text{constant}$$

Chapter XII

Important Formulae : Heat and Thermometry

1. Heat supplied to (or taken out of) a substance:

$$Q = C\Delta T = C(T_2 - T_1)$$

2. Heat supplied in terms of molar heat capacity:

$$Q = nC_m\Delta T = nC_m(T_2 - T_1)$$

where C_m is the molar heat capacity.

3. Ratio of specific heats:

$$\gamma = \frac{C_p}{C_V}$$

and

$$C_p - C_V = R$$

4. $^\circ F = \frac{9}{5}{}^\circ C + 32,\ K = 273.15 + {}^\circ C, {}^\circ R = {}^\circ F + 459.67, {}^\circ R = \frac{9}{5} K$

5. $\alpha = \frac{dL}{L_0 dT}, \beta = \frac{dA}{A_0 dT}$ and $\gamma = \frac{dV}{V_0 dT}$

6. $I = I_0(1 + \alpha T), A = A_0(1 + \beta T)$ and $V = V_0(1 + \gamma T)$

7. $\alpha = \frac{\beta}{2} = \frac{\gamma}{3}$

8. Heat energy $Q = K\frac{A(\theta_1 - \theta_2)t}{d}$, where temperature gradient $= \frac{(\theta_1 - \theta_2)}{d}$

Chapter XIII

References

1. H. C. Verma, *Concepts of Physics, Part 1 and 2*, Bharati Bhawan Publishers, 2004.

2. National Council of Educational Research and Training, *Physics, Class XI*, NCERT, 2006.

3. National Council of Educational Research and Training, *Physics, Class XII*, NCERT, 2007.

4. D. Halliday, R. Resnick, and J. Walker, *Fundamentals of Physics*, 10th ed., Wiley, 2013.

5. P. Tipler and G. Mosca, *Physics for Scientists and Engineers*, 6th ed., W. H. Freeman, 2007.

6. H. D. Young and R. A. Freedman, *University Physics with Modern Physics*, 14th ed., Pearson, 2015.

7. R. A. Serway and J. W. Jewett, *Physics for Scientists and Engineers*, 9th ed., Cengage Learning, 2013.

8. S. Satya Prakash, *Advanced Physics for Class XII*, Pragati Prakashan, 2001.

9. K. S. Krane, *Modern Physics*, 3rd ed., Wiley, 2012.

10. F. W. Sears, M. W. Zemansky, and H. D. Young, *University Physics*, 11th ed., Pearson, 2003.

Applied Physics-II: Practice Questions and Answers

Applied Physics-II: Practice Questions and Answers

For Diploma Engineering Students as per AICTE new syllabus

by

Bikash Kumar Naik

Published by Notion Press

Preface

The study of physics provides a vital foundation for engineering and technical education, equipping students with fundamental concepts that bridge theoretical understanding and real-world applications. This book, *Applied Physics-II: Practice Questions and Answers for Diploma Engineering Students*, has been meticulously crafted to align with the latest AICTE syllabus, offering a clear and structured approach to applied physics.

Each unit begins with essential theoretical principles, followed by an extensive selection of practice questions that cover both theoretical and practical aspects. Detailed answers and step-by-step solutions are provided to support independent study, enabling students to review and solidify their knowledge effectively.

Covering key areas like wave motion, optics, electrostatics, current electricity, electromagnetism, and semiconductor physics, this book serves as a comprehensive resource for students aiming to build a strong foundation in physics. Through engagement with these topics, students will not only enhance their exam preparation but also develop a deeper appreciation of physics' role in various engineering challenges.

It is my hope that this book will be a valuable tool for students, fostering both confidence and proficiency as they advance in their studies.

Bikash Kumar Naik

Contents

Chapter I

Unit-1 : Wave motion and its applications

2 Marks Questions & Solutions

Q-1: Define wave motion and distinguish between transverse and longitudinal waves with an example for each.
Ans: A wave is a disturbance that transfers energy from one place to another without transferring matter. In transverse waves, particles of the medium move perpendicular to the direction of wave propagation (e.g., light waves), while in longitudinal waves, particles move parallel to the direction of propagation (e.g., sound waves in air).

Q-2: Explain the term wave velocity and provide its SI unit.
Ans: Wave velocity is the speed at which the wave propagates through a medium. It is defined as the distance traveled by a crest or trough per unit time and is measured in meters per second (m/s).

Q-3: State the relationship between wave velocity (v), frequency (f), and wavelength (λ).
Ans: The relationship is given by the equation $v = f\lambda$, where v is the wave velocity, f is the frequency, and λ is the wavelength.

Q-4: What is the principle of superposition of waves? Provide an example.
Ans: The principle of superposition states that when two or more waves overlap, the resultant displacement at any point is the sum of the displacements due to individual waves. An example is the formation of constructive and destructive interference patterns.

Q-5: What is the phase of a wave? How is it different from phase difference?
Ans: The phase of a wave represents the state of motion of the wave at a particular point in time. The phase difference between two waves is the amount by which one wave is ahead or behind the other in terms of their oscillatory motion.

Q-6: A wave has a frequency of 100 Hz and a wavelength of 2 m. Calculate its wave velocity.
Ans: Using $v = f\lambda$, wave velocity $v = 100\,\text{Hz} \times 2\,\text{m} = 200\,\text{m/s}$.

Q-7: If the wave equation is given by $y = 5\sin(3x - 4t)$, identify the amplitude and angular frequency of the wave.
Ans: The amplitude is 5 units, and the angular frequency is 4 rad/s.

Q-8: Two sound waves of frequencies 256 Hz and 260 Hz are played simultaneously. What is the beat frequency produced?

Ans: The beat frequency is given by $|f_1 - f_2| = |260 - 256| = 4\,\text{Hz}$.

Q-9: What is the wavelength of a sound wave in air with a speed of 340 m/s and a frequency of 170 Hz?

Ans: Using $v = f\lambda$, $\lambda = \frac{v}{f} = \frac{340\,\text{m/s}}{170\,\text{Hz}} = 2\,\text{m}$.

Q-10: Describe the properties of light waves that distinguish them from sound waves.

Ans: Light waves are electromagnetic, can travel in a vacuum, and exhibit properties like reflection, refraction, and diffraction. Sound waves are mechanical, require a medium to travel, and are longitudinal in nature.

Q-11: Explain beat formation with an example in sound waves.

Ans: Beats are formed when two sound waves of slightly different frequencies interfere, resulting in periodic variations in amplitude. For example, tuning two musical instruments to achieve a consistent frequency reduces the beats.

Q-12: A wave traveling in a medium has a phase difference of $\pi/4$ between two points. What is the path difference if the wavelength is 8 cm?

Ans: Path difference $= \left(\frac{\text{Phase difference}}{2\pi}\right) \times \text{Wavelength} = \left(\frac{\pi/4}{2\pi}\right) \times 8\,\text{cm} = 1\,\text{cm}$.

Q-13: If the amplitude of a wave doubles, what effect does it have on the energy transported by the wave?

Ans: The energy transported by a wave is proportional to the square of its amplitude. Doubling the amplitude increases the energy by a factor of four.

Q-14: Differentiate between transverse and longitudinal wave properties in terms of particle movement and example mediums.

Ans: In transverse waves, particles move perpendicular to wave direction (e.g., water surface waves), while in longitudinal waves, particles move parallel (e.g., sound in air).

Q-15. Define forced vibrations and resonance. Provide an example for each.

Ans.

- **Forced Vibrations:** Forced vibrations occur when a system is driven by an external periodic force. The frequency of the driving force is different from the natural frequency of the system. Example: A child on a swing pushed periodically.

- **Resonance:** Resonance occurs when the frequency of the externally applied force matches the natural frequency of the system, resulting in large amplitude oscillations. Example: Pushing a swing at the right intervals.

(5 MARKS QUESTIONS & SOLUTIONS)

Q1. Explain the difference between transverse and longitudinal waves. Describe their characteristics and give an example of each type of wave.
Answer:

- **Transverse Waves:** Transverse waves are waves in which the particle motion is **perpendicular** to the direction of wave propagation. In such waves, crests and troughs are formed.

    – Example: Light waves or waves on a string.

    – Characteristics:

        * Particles move **up and down** relative to the direction of wave propagation.

        * Can travel through **solids and surfaces**.

        * Distance between corresponding particles does not change as vibrations are perpendicular.

- **Longitudinal Waves:** Longitudinal waves are waves in which particle motion is **parallel** to the direction of wave propagation. In such waves, compressions and rarefactions are formed.

    – Example: Sound waves in air.

    – Characteristics:

        * Particles move **back and forth** along the direction of wave propagation.

        * Can travel through **solids, liquids, and gases**.

        * Distance between corresponding particles changes as the wave propagates due to compressions (particles closer together) and rarefactions (particles farther apart).

When a wave passes through a medium, the particles of the medium vibrate about their mean position. If the direction of vibration is **perpendicular** to the wave's travel, the wave is a **transverse wave**. If the vibration is **along** the wave's travel, the wave is a **longitudinal wave**.

For example:

- In a wave traveling along a string, the disturbance is perpendicular to the length of the string, resembling a transverse wave.

- In a wave traveling along a spring, the disturbance is along the length of the spring, resembling a longitudinal wave.

Figure 1.1 illustrates the relative positions of particles in transverse and longitudinal waves. In both cases:

- Particles reach maximum displacement during vibration and return to their mean position before moving to the opposite extreme.

- The **maximum** and **minimum** positions in transverse waves are called **crest** and **trough**, respectively.

- In longitudinal waves, the **compression** corresponds to the crest, and the **rarefaction** corresponds to the trough of transverse waves.

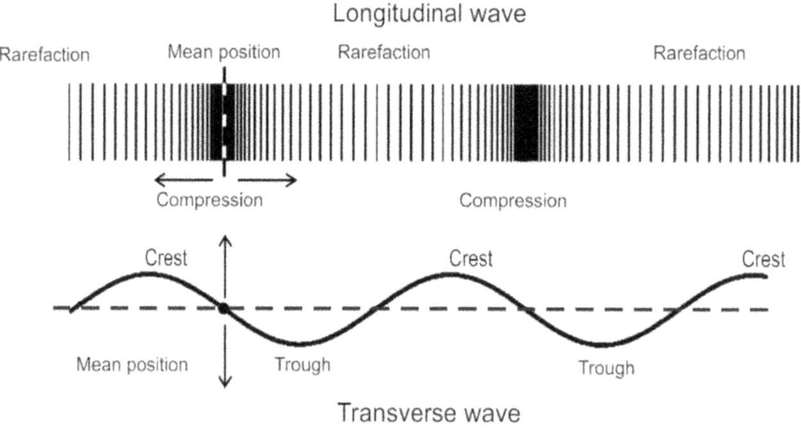

Figure 1.1: Representation of transverse and longitudinal waves.

Q2. Define wave velocity, frequency, and wavelength. Derive the relationship between these quantities.

Ans.

- **Wave Velocity (v):** Wave velocity is the speed at which the wave propagates through a medium. It is measured in meters per second (m/s).

- **Frequency (f):** Frequency is the number of oscillations per unit time. It is measured in hertz (Hz).

- **Wavelength (λ):** Wavelength is the distance between two consecutive crests or troughs in a transverse wave or between two compressions in a longitudinal wave. It is measured in meters (m).

- **Relationship:** The wave velocity is related to frequency and wavelength by the formula:

$$v = f\lambda$$

  where v is the wave velocity, f is the frequency, and λ is the wavelength.

Q3. Discuss the properties of sound and light waves and distinguish between them based on their propagation and medium requirements.

Ans.

- **Sound Waves:**

    - Sound waves are mechanical, longitudinal waves.

    - They require a medium (solid, liquid, or gas) to propagate, as they are caused by particle vibrations.

    - The speed of sound is approximately 340 m/s in air at room temperature, but it varies in different media.

- **Light Waves:**

    - Light waves are electromagnetic, transverse waves.

    - They do not require a medium and can travel through a vacuum, as they consist of oscillating electric and magnetic fields.

    - The speed of light in a vacuum is approximately 3×10^8 m/s.

- **Key Differences:**

    - Sound waves are longitudinal, while light waves are transverse.

    - Sound waves need a medium to travel, but light waves can travel in a vacuum.

Q4. Explain the principle of superposition of waves and describe how it leads to the phenomenon of beats.

Ans.

- **Principle of Superposition:** The **principle of superposition** states that when two or more waves overlap, the resultant displacement at any point is the sum of the displacements due to each individual wave. Mathematically, if two waves are represented as

$$y_1 = a_1 \sin(\omega t) \quad \text{and} \quad y_2 = a_2 \sin(\omega t + \phi),$$

  then the resultant displacement is

$$y = y_1 + y_2 = a_1 \sin(\omega t) + a_2 \sin(\omega t + \phi).$$

- **Resultant Displacement:** Let the first and second waves have the same frequency and be represented as:

$$y_1 = a_1 \sin(\omega t) \quad \text{and} \quad y_2 = a_2 \sin(\omega t + \phi),$$

  where ϕ is the phase difference between the two waves.

  The resultant displacement is given by:

$$y = y_1 + y_2 = a_1 \sin(\omega t) + a_2 \sin(\omega t + \phi).$$

  Using the trigonometric identity for $\sin(\omega t + \phi)$, we can expand the second term:

$$y = a_1 \sin(\omega t) + a_2[\sin(\omega t)\cos(\phi) + \cos(\omega t)\sin(\phi)].$$

  This simplifies to:

$$y = \sin(\omega t)[a_1 + a_2 \cos(\phi)] + a_2 \cos(\omega t)\sin(\phi).$$

  Let:

$$a_1 + a_2 \cos(\phi) = a' \cos(\alpha) \quad \text{and} \quad a_2 \sin(\phi) = a' \sin(\alpha),$$

  where a' and α are new amplitude and phase terms, respectively.

  Substituting these into the expression for y, we get:

$$y = \sin(\omega t)a' \cos(\alpha) + \cos(\omega t)a' \sin(\alpha),$$

  which simplifies to:

$$y = a' \sin(\omega t + \alpha).$$

  Thus, the resultant amplitude due to the superposition of the two waves at any point is a', and the frequency is the same as that of the combining waves.

- **Beat Formation:** When two waves of slightly different frequencies interfere, they produce a phenomenon called **beats**, where the amplitude of the resultant wave oscillates with time. The resultant wave can be expressed as:

$$y = A\sin(\omega t),$$

where $A = 2a\cos\left(\frac{(\omega_1 - \omega_2)t}{2}\right)$, and the frequency ω is the average of the two frequencies ω_1 and ω_2.

- **Mathematical Representation:** Let us consider two waves with the same amplitude $a_1 = a_2 = a$ and phase difference $\phi = 0$. The displacement of the two waves is given by:

$$y = a_1 \sin(\omega_1 t) + a_2 \sin(\omega_2 t + \phi).$$

For $\phi = 0$ and $a_1 = a_2 = a$, the displacement becomes:

$$y = a\sin(\omega_1 t) + a\sin(\omega_2 t).$$

This can be rewritten as:

$$y = 2a\sin\left(\frac{\omega_1 + \omega_2}{2}t\right)\cos\left(\frac{\omega_1 - \omega_2}{2}t\right).$$

As the two frequencies are slightly different, we approximate the average frequency $\omega \approx \frac{\omega_1 + \omega_2}{2}$. This gives the resultant wave as:

$$y = A\sin(\omega t),$$

where $A = 2a\cos\left(\frac{\omega_1 - \omega_2}{2}t\right)$ represents the amplitude of the beat wave, and ω is the average angular frequency of the two waves.

- **Beat Period:** The beat period T_b is the time interval between two consecutive maxima of the resultant wave. The beat period can be calculated by determining when the amplitude A reaches a maximum. For the amplitude to be maximum, we require:

$$\cos\left(\frac{(\omega_1 - \omega_2)t}{2}\right) = \pm 1.$$

This occurs when:

$$\frac{(\omega_1 - \omega_2)t}{2} = n\pi, \quad \text{for} \quad n = 0, 1, 2, 3, \ldots$$

For $n = 0$, we have $t = 0$, which corresponds to the first maximum at $t = 0$. Therefore, the beat period T_b is given by:

$$T_b = \frac{2\pi}{\omega_1 - \omega_2}.$$

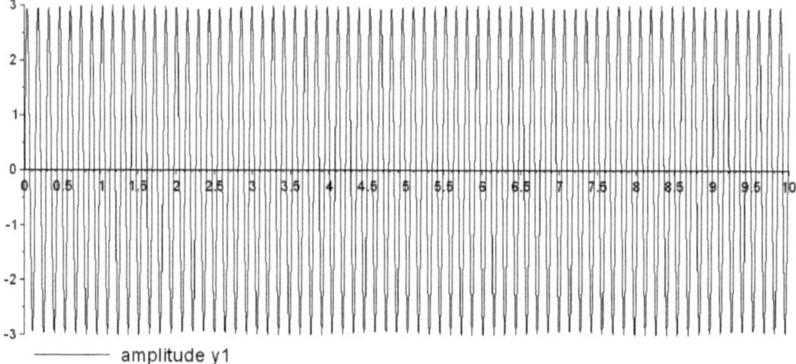

Figure I.2: $y_1 = 3\sin(2\pi v_1 t - k_1 x)$ with $v_1 = 9.5$ and $k_1 = 15$.

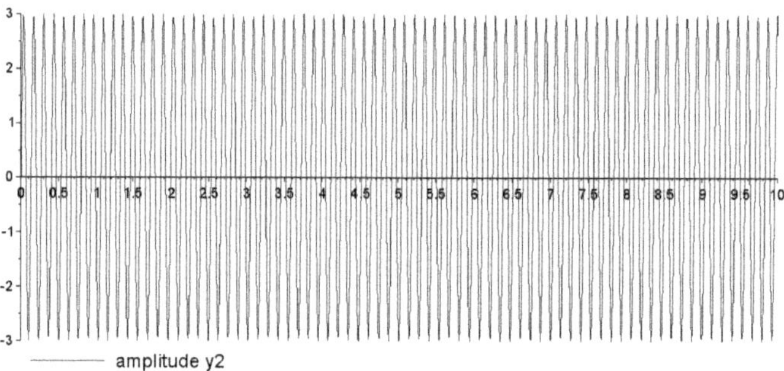

Figure I.3: $y_2 = 3\sin(2\pi v_2 t - k_2 x)$ with $v_2 = 10$ and $k_2 = 15.5$.

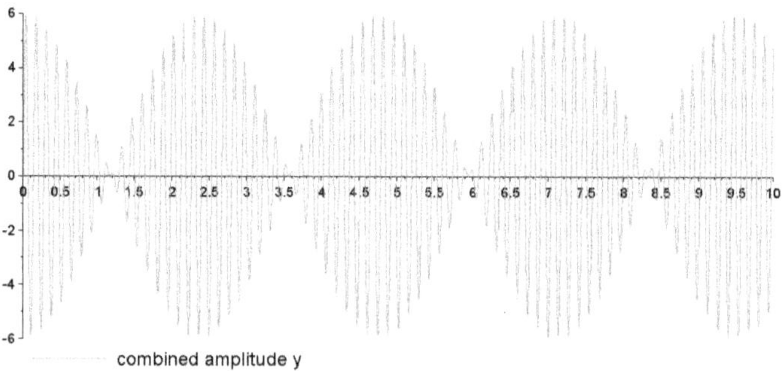

Figure I.4: Superposition of the two waves $y = y_1 + y_2$; beat formation.

- **Beat Frequency:** The beat frequency f_b is the difference in frequency between the two interfering waves. If the frequencies of the two waves are f_1 and f_2, then the beat frequency is given by:

$$f_b = |f_1 - f_2|.$$

The beat period T_b is the time between two consecutive maxima of the resultant wave, and is given by:

$$T_b = \frac{1}{f_b}.$$

- **Observation:** This phenomenon is commonly observed in sound waves when two musical notes with slightly different frequencies are played together. The result is a pulsing sound that fluctuates in loudness, known as the **beats**.

Q5. Given the wave equation $y = A\sin(\omega t + \phi)$**, explain the terms amplitude, phase, and phase difference. How do these quantities affect wave motion?**

Ans.

- **Amplitude (A):** The amplitude is the maximum displacement of particles from their equilibrium position. It determines the energy carried by the wave; higher amplitude means higher energy.

- **Phase (ϕ):** The phase represents the initial angle or starting point of the wave at $t = 0$. It determines the starting position of the wave motion.

- **Phase Difference:** The phase difference between two waves is the amount by which one wave is ahead or behind another. It affects constructive or destructive interference between waves.

- **Effect on Wave Motion:**

    - A larger amplitude results in more energetic waves.

    - The phase determines where the wave starts in its cycle.

    - A phase difference between two waves can lead to interference patterns.

    - **Q6. A wave has a frequency of 50 Hz and a wavelength of 2 m. Calculate its wave velocity.**

    - **Solution:** The wave velocity v is given by the relation:

$$v = f\lambda$$

    where:

$$\frac{d^2y}{dt^2} = -w^2 y$$

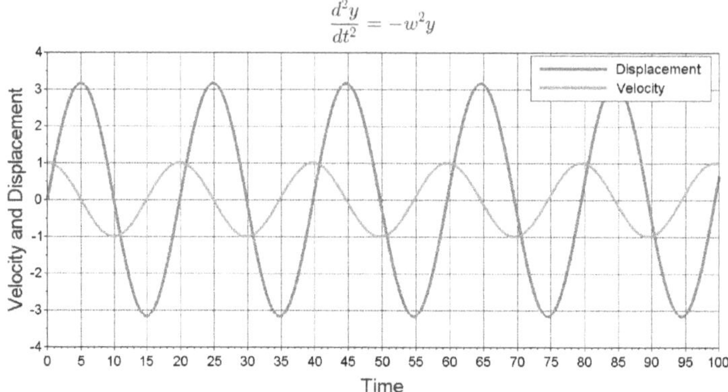

Figure I.5: Variation of velocity and displacement with time for free oscillations with $m = 0.1\,\text{kg}$, $k = 0.01\,\text{N/m}$, and $\omega = 0.316\,\text{s}^{-1}$ for $y = 0$ and $\frac{dy}{dt} = 1$ at $t = 0$. Fig. 1 shows how velocity and displacement vary with time: for free oscillation, displacement varies as a sine function and velocity as a cosine function, with a relative phase difference of $90°$.

$$* \quad f = 50\,\text{Hz (frequency)}$$

$$* \quad \lambda = 2\,\text{m (wavelength)}$$

Substituting the values:

$$v = 50\,\text{Hz} \times 2\,\text{m} = 100\,\text{m/s}$$

Thus, the wave velocity is $100\,\text{m/s}$.

- **Q6. Define Simple Harmonic Motion (SHM) and derive the expression for its displacement.**

Ans.

- **Definition of SHM:** Simple Harmonic Motion is a type of periodic motion in which the restoring force is directly proportional to the displacement and acts in the opposite direction. The motion occurs along a straight line, and the displacement varies sinusoidally with time.

- **Expression for Displacement:** The displacement of a body undergoing SHM is given by:

$$y(t) = A\sin(\omega t + \phi)$$

where:

* A is the amplitude (maximum displacement),

* ω is the angular frequency,

* t is time,

* ϕ is the phase constant.

- **Q7. What is the time period and frequency of a simple harmonic oscillator? Derive the relation between them.**

Ans.

- **Time Period:** The time period T is the time taken to complete one full oscillation. For SHM, the time period is given by:

$$T = \frac{2\pi}{\omega}$$

where ω is the angular frequency.

- **Frequency:** The frequency f is the number of oscillations per unit time. It is related to the time period by:

$$f = \frac{1}{T} = \frac{\omega}{2\pi}$$

Therefore, the frequency is the reciprocal of the time period.

- **Q8. Explain the concept of Simple Harmonic Motion (SHM) and derive the expressions for velocity and acceleration. Also, explain the energy transfer in SHM.**

Ans.

- **Concept of SHM:** Simple Harmonic Motion is a type of oscillatory motion where the restoring force is proportional to the displacement from the equilibrium position and acts in the opposite direction. This motion is characterized by sinusoidal displacement over time.

- **Expression for Velocity:** The velocity in SHM is the time derivative of displacement $x(t) = A\sin(\omega t + \phi)$:

$$v(t) = A\omega \cos(\omega t + \phi)$$

- **Expression for Acceleration:** The acceleration is the time derivative of velocity:

$$a(t) = -A\omega^2 \sin(\omega t + \phi)$$

  which is proportional to the displacement and directed opposite to it.

- **Energy Transfer in SHM:** The total mechanical energy in SHM is constant and is the sum of kinetic and potential energy:

$$E_{\text{total}} = \frac{1}{2}m\omega^2 A^2$$

  The energy oscillates between kinetic and potential forms as the body moves through the motion.

- **Question: Explain the concept of Simple Harmonic Motion (SHM), derive the expressions for velocity and acceleration, and explain the energy transfer in SHM. Also, provide an example of SHM in a cantilever beam and derive its time period.**

  Answer:

  - **1. Concept of Simple Harmonic Motion (SHM)**

    Simple Harmonic Motion (SHM) is a type of periodic motion in which the restoring force acting on a body is directly proportional to the displacement of the body from its equilibrium position and acts in the opposite direction. This type of motion is characterized by sinusoidal oscillations, meaning the displacement, velocity, and acceleration of the particle follow sine or cosine functions over time.

    Key characteristics of SHM:

    * The restoring force F is proportional to displacement y (Hooke's Law):

    $$F = -ky$$

      where k is the spring constant or force constant, and y is the displacement.

    * The motion is oscillatory, meaning the body moves back and forth about the equilibrium position.

    * The displacement, velocity, and acceleration of the body vary sinusoidally with time.

— 2. Derivation of Expressions for Velocity and Acceleration in SHM

For SHM, the displacement as a function of time is typically written as:

$$y(t) = A \sin(\omega t + \phi)$$

where:

* A is the amplitude of the oscillation (maximum displacement),

* ω is the angular frequency ($\omega = 2\pi f$), related to the frequency f,

* ϕ is the phase constant, which depends on the initial conditions.

a. Velocity Expression:

Velocity is the rate of change of displacement. To find the velocity, differentiate the displacement $x(t)$ with respect to time:

$$v(t) = \frac{dy(t)}{dt} = A\omega \sin(\omega t + \phi)$$

This equation shows that the velocity is sinusoidal and reaches its maximum value at the equilibrium position (when $x = 0$) and zero at the extreme positions (when $x = \pm A$).

b. Acceleration Expression:

Acceleration is the rate of change of velocity. Differentiate the velocity expression with respect to time:

$$a(t) = \frac{dv(t)}{dt} = -A\omega^2 \cos(\omega t + \phi)$$

This shows that acceleration is also sinusoidal, and it is always directed towards the equilibrium position. The maximum acceleration occurs at the extreme points of the motion, where the displacement is maximum ($x = \pm A$).

Hence, the acceleration in SHM is given by:

$$a(t) = -\omega^2 y(t)$$

This shows that the acceleration is proportional to the displacement, but in the opposite direction (restoring force).

— 3. Energy Transfer in SHM

The total mechanical energy in SHM remains constant throughout the motion, and it is the sum of two types of energy: kinetic energy (KE) and potential energy (PE).

a. Kinetic Energy (KE):

The kinetic energy of the particle is given by:

$$KE = \frac{1}{2}mv^2$$

Substitute the expression for velocity $v(t) = A\omega \cos(\omega t + \phi)$:

$$KE = \frac{1}{2}mA^2\omega^2 \cos^2(\omega t + \phi)$$

The kinetic energy is maximum when the particle passes through the equilibrium position (where $\cos(\omega t + \phi) = \pm 1$) and zero when the particle is at the extreme positions (where $\cos(\omega t + \phi) = 0$).

b. Potential Energy (PE):

The potential energy in SHM is stored due to the displacement from the equilibrium position. It is given by:

$$PE = \frac{1}{2}ky^2$$

Substitute $y(t) = A \sin(\omega t + \phi)$ into this equation:

$$PE = \frac{1}{2}kA^2 \sin^2(\omega t + \phi)$$

The potential energy is maximum at the extreme positions (where $\sin(\omega t + \phi) = \pm 1$) and zero at the equilibrium position (where $\sin(\omega t + \phi) = 0$).

c. Total Energy:

The total mechanical energy E_{total} in SHM is the sum of the kinetic and potential energy:

$$E_{\text{total}} = KE + PE$$

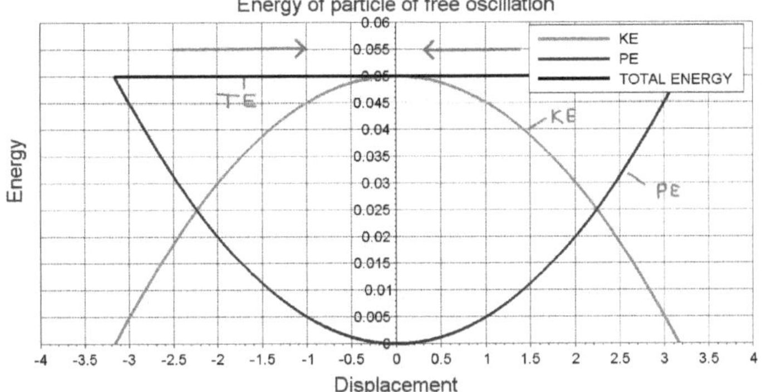

Figure I.6: Variation of kinetic energy, potential energy, and total energy with displacement for free oscillation with $k = 0.01$ N/m and $m = 0.1$ kg for $y = 0$ and velocity $\frac{dy}{dt} = 1$ at $t = 0$.FigI. 2. shows that the total energy is constant for free oscillation. At the two extreme points, the kinetic energy is zero, i.e., the oscillator's velocity changes direction, and the potential energy is maximum. At the equilibrium position, the kinetic energy is maximum, the potential energy is minimum, and both functions can be seen to be parabolic.

Since energy is transferred between kinetic and potential forms during the motion, the total energy remains constant over time:

$$E_{\text{total}} = \frac{1}{2}mA^2\omega^2$$

This shows that the total energy is constant and independent of time. It only depends on the mass m, amplitude A, and angular frequency ω.

— 4. Example: SHM in a Cantilever Beam

A cantilever beam is a system in which one end is fixed, and a mass is attached at the free end. When the mass is displaced slightly and released, the beam undergoes simple harmonic motion.

a. Time Period of SHM in Cantilever Beam:

The time period of oscillation of the cantilever can be derived using the following formula for the time period T of SHM:

$$T = 2\pi\sqrt{\frac{m}{k}}$$

where:

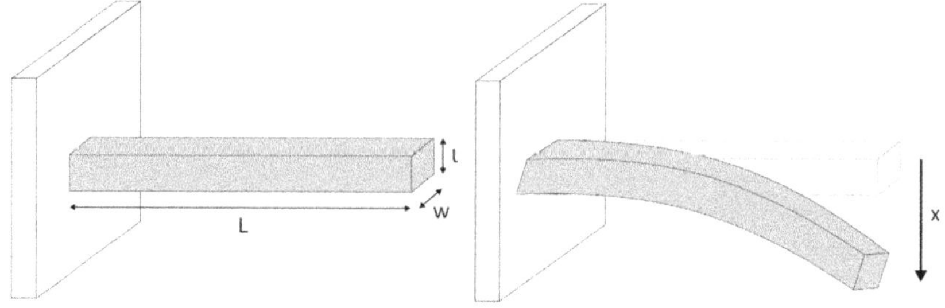

Figure I.7: Vibration of cantilever

* m is the mass attached at the free end,

* k is the stiffness of the cantilever.

The stiffness k of a cantilever beam is related to the material's Young's modulus E, the moment of inertia I, and the length L of the beam:

$$k = \frac{3EI}{L^3}$$

where:

* E is Young's modulus of the material,

* I is the moment of inertia of the beam's cross-sectional area. For a rectangular beam, I is given by:

$$I = \frac{1}{12}wt^3$$

where w is the width and t is the thickness of the beam.

Thus, the time period of SHM for the cantilever beam is:

$$T = 2\pi\sqrt{\frac{mL^3}{3EI}}$$

Substitute I for a rectangular beam:

$$T = 2\pi\sqrt{\frac{mL^3}{3E\left(\frac{1}{12}wt^3\right)}}$$

Simplifying further:

$$T = 2\pi\sqrt{\frac{12mL^3}{3Ewt^3}}$$

$$T = 2\pi\sqrt{\frac{4mL^3}{Ewt^3}}$$

This equation gives the time period of the oscillation for a cantilever beam performing SHM.

— **Q2. Discuss the vibration of a cantilever and derive the expression for its time period. Also, explain the concept of resonance with an example.**

Ans.

* **Vibration of a Cantilever:** A cantilever is a beam fixed at one end and free at the other. When the free end is displaced and released, it vibrates with a certain natural frequency. The time period of the vibration is given by:

$$T = 2\pi\sqrt{\frac{I}{mgh}}$$

where I is the moment of inertia, m is the mass of the cantilever, g is the acceleration due to gravity, and h is the length of the cantilever.

* **Resonance:** Resonance occurs when the frequency of an externally applied force matches the natural frequency of a system, causing large amplitude oscillations. An example of resonance is pushing a swing at the right intervals to make it go higher.

— **Q3. What are the acoustics of buildings? Discuss reverberation, echo, and methods to control reverberation time.**

Ans.

* **Acoustics of Buildings:** Acoustics is the study of sound in buildings. It deals with the reflection, absorption, and transmission of sound to ensure good sound quality within a space, such as in theaters and concert halls.

* **Reverberation:** Reverberation is the persistence of sound in a space due to the repeated reflection of sound waves from surfaces. It can cause poor speech intelligibility if excessive.

* **Echo:** An echo is the reflection of sound from a distant surface, heard after a delay. This happens when sound waves travel long distances and reflect off surfaces such as walls or mountains.

* **Methods to Control Reverberation:** Reverberation time can be controlled by using sound-absorbing materials like carpets, curtains, and acoustic panels. In large halls, designing the room shape and using materials that absorb sound waves effectively helps in controlling reverberation time.

– **Q4. Explain the properties and applications of ultrasonic waves.**
Answer:

* **Properties of Ultrasonic Waves:**

  · Ultrasonic waves are sound waves with frequencies above $20,000$ Hz, which is beyond the audible range of human hearing.
  · They have a **high frequency**, **short wavelength**, and **high energy**.
  · Ultrasonic waves can travel through solids, liquids, and gases with minimal attenuation.
  · Animals like bats and dolphins use ultrasonic waves for navigation and detecting obstacles.

* **Applications of Ultrasonic Waves:**

  · **Medical Applications:**
  · **Ultrasound Scanning:** Used in sonography for medical diagnosis, such as imaging organs and scanning fetuses during pregnancy. The frequency range of diagnostic sonography is $2\,\text{MHz}$ to $18\,\text{MHz}$.

  · **Engineering Applications:**
  · **Non-Destructive Testing (NDT):** Detects cracks and defects in metals and other materials. Ultrasound waves are reflected from cracks, allowing detection without damaging the object.

  · **Sound Navigation and Ranging (SONAR):** Used in submarines to detect nearby objects and measure sea depth. The distance is calculated using:

  $$\text{Time of Flight} = \frac{2 \times \text{Distance}}{\text{Velocity of Sound in Water}}$$

· **Position Sensors:** Used in modern sensors to measure distances by calculating the time of flight of ultrasonic waves. Temperature variations are considered for accurate calculations.

· **Industrial Applications:**

· **Ultrasonication:** Used to speed up chemical reactions, clean equipment, and remove air bubbles in reaction chambers by generating alternating low- and high-pressure waves.

Illustrations:

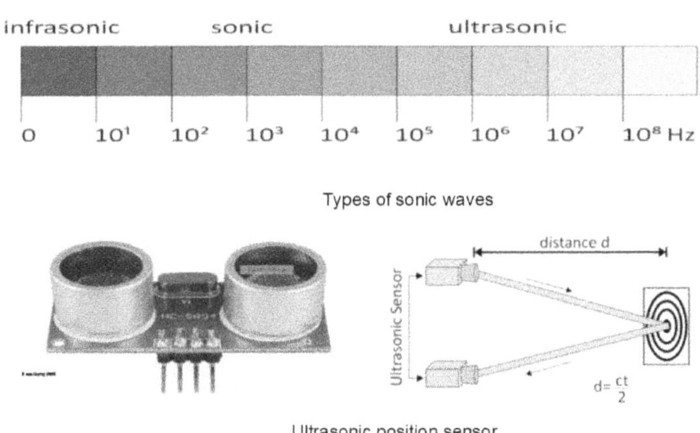

Figure I.8: Applications of Ultrasonic Waves.

— **Q5. Explain the differences between sound waves and light waves. Discuss their properties.**

Answer:

* **Nature of Waves:**

· **Sound Waves:** Sound waves are **mechanical waves** that require a medium (solid, liquid, or gas) for propagation. They cannot travel in a vacuum.

- **Light Waves:** Light waves are **electromagnetic waves** that do not require a medium. They can propagate in a vacuum.

* **Wave Classification:**

  - **Sound Waves:** They can be **longitudinal** or **transverse**, but in air, sound waves are **longitudinal**.

  - **Light Waves:** Light waves are always **transverse**. They exhibit oscillations of electric and magnetic field vectors perpendicular to the direction of wave propagation.

* **Velocity of Propagation:**

  - **Sound Waves:** The velocity of sound depends on the medium. For example, in air at 20°C, the velocity is approximately 340 m/s. The velocity changes with the density of air and other physical properties of the medium.

  - **Light Waves:** The velocity of light in a vacuum or air is approximately 3×10^8 m/s. The velocity decreases when light propagates through a medium.

* **Key Characteristics:**

  - **Sound Waves:**

  - Comprised of **compressions** (high pressure) and **rarefactions** (low pressure) due to their longitudinal nature.

  - The velocity is influenced by temperature, pressure, and density of the medium.

  - **Light Waves:**

  - Exhibit variations in **electric** and **magnetic** field vectors.

  - Light can be polarized due to its transverse nature.

Equations of Wave Properties:

* Velocity of a wave: $v = f\lambda$, where:

- v: Wave velocity.

- f: Frequency.

- λ: Wavelength.

* Frequency and time period relation: $f = \frac{1}{T}$, where T is the time period of the wave.

Chapter II

Unit-2 : Optics

Unit-II: 2 Marks Questions & Solutions

- **Q1. State the laws of reflection and refraction.**

  Ans.

  - **Laws of Reflection:**

    * The angle of incidence is equal to the angle of reflection ($i = r$).

    * The incident ray, the reflected ray, and the normal to the surface at the point of incidence all lie in the same plane.

  - **Laws of Refraction:**

    * The ratio of the sine of the angle of incidence (i) to the sine of the angle of refraction (r) is constant and is called the refractive index (n):
    $$\frac{\sin i}{\sin r} = n$$

    * The incident ray, the refracted ray, and the normal at the point of incidence all lie in the same plane.

- **Q2. Define the refractive index and derive the relation between refractive index and speed of light.**

  Ans.

  - **Refractive Index:** The refractive index (n) of a medium is the ratio of the speed of light in a vacuum (c) to the speed of light in the medium (v):
  $$n = \frac{c}{v}$$

  where:

* c is the speed of light in a vacuum,

* v is the speed of light in the medium.

- **Q3. What is the lens formula? Derive the expression for the focal length of a lens.**

Ans.

- **Lens Formula:** The lens formula is:

$$\frac{1}{f} = \frac{1}{v} - \frac{1}{u}$$

where:

* f is the focal length,

* v is the image distance,

* u is the object distance.

- **Derivation for Focal Length:** The lens formula is derived using the geometry of the lens and the concept of refraction. For a converging lens:

$$\frac{1}{f} = \frac{1}{v} - \frac{1}{u}$$

This equation relates the focal length of the lens to the distances of the object and the image formed.

- **Q4. What is the magnifying power of a microscope?**

Ans.

- **Magnifying Power of a Microscope:** The magnifying power (M) of a simple microscope is defined as the ratio of the angular size of the object when viewed through the microscope to the angular size when viewed with the naked eye. It is given by:

$$M = \frac{D}{f}$$

where:

* D is the least distance of distinct vision (usually taken as 25 cm),

* f is the focal length of the lens.

Unit-II: 5 Marks Questions & Solutions

- **Q1. Derive the lens formula and explain its application in finding the image formed by a lens. Also, explain the power of a lens.**

Ans.

- **Lens Formula:** The lens formula is derived using the principles of refraction at a spherical surface and the geometry of the lens. It relates the object distance u, the image distance v, and the focal length f of the lens:

$$\frac{1}{f} = \frac{1}{v} - \frac{1}{u}$$

- **Application of Lens Formula:** The lens formula can be used to find the image formed by a lens when the object distance and focal length are known. For example, if the object is placed beyond the focal point of a converging lens, a real and inverted image is formed.

- **Power of a Lens:** The power of a lens is defined as the reciprocal of its focal length f (in meters):

$$P = \frac{1}{f}$$

The unit of power is diopters (D). A converging lens has a positive power, and a diverging lens has a negative power.

- **Q2. A ray of light passes from air (refractive index = 1) into water (refractive index = 1.33). If the angle of incidence in air is 30°, find the angle of refraction in water.**

Ans.

- **Given:** Refractive index of air $n_1 = 1$, refractive index of water $n_2 = 1.33$, angle of incidence in air $i = 30°$.

- **Solution:** Using Snell's law:

$$n_1 \sin i = n_2 \sin r$$

Substituting the known values:

$$1 \times \sin 30° = 1.33 \times \sin r$$

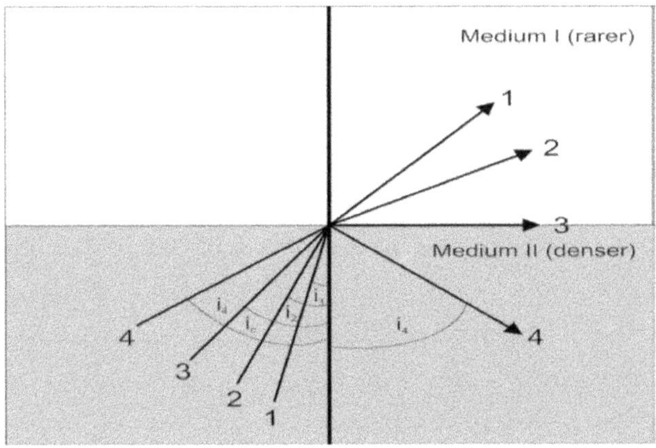

Figure II.1: Total internal reflection

$$\sin r = \frac{\sin 30^\circ}{1.33} = \frac{0.5}{1.33} \approx 0.375$$

$$r = \sin^{-1}(0.375) \approx 22.02^\circ$$

Therefore, the angle of refraction in water is approximately 22.02°.

- **Q3. Explain the phenomenon of total internal reflection and derive the expression for the critical angle. Discuss its applications in optical fibers.**

Ans.

- **Total Internal Reflection:** Total internal reflection occurs when a ray of light travels from a denser medium to a rarer medium, and the angle of incidence exceeds a certain critical angle. In this case, all the light is reflected back into the denser medium.

- **Critical Angle:** The critical angle C is the angle of incidence at which the angle of refraction is 90°. Using Snell's law:

$$n_1 \sin C = n_2 \sin 90^\circ$$

Since $\sin 90^\circ = 1$, we get:

$$\sin C = \frac{n_2}{n_1}$$

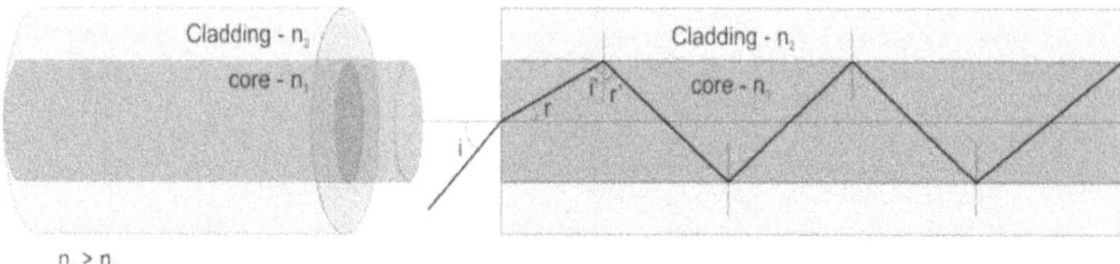

Figure II.2: TIR in optical fiber

— **Examples of Total Internal Reflection (TIR):** Some common examples of TIR are:

  * **Shining of a Diamond:** A diamond sparkles due to total internal reflection. The light entering the diamond undergoes multiple reflections inside the diamond before emerging, creating the characteristic sparkle.

  * **Formation of Mirage:** A mirage is an optical illusion caused by total internal reflection. In hot weather, light bends due to temperature gradients in the air, causing TIR at different layers of air and making distant objects appear closer or distorted.

  * **Periscope:** A periscope uses total internal reflection to allow users to view objects from around corners. Light reflects off mirrors at angles that ensure total internal reflection, guiding the light to the viewer's eyes.

— **Applications in Optical Fibers:** Optical fibers use total internal reflection to transmit light signals over long distances with minimal loss. The core of the fiber has a higher refractive index than the surrounding cladding, ensuring total internal reflection of light traveling through the fiber.

- **Q4. Explain the working of a simple microscope and derive the expression for its magnifying power.**

Ans.

- **Working of a Simple Microscope:** A simple microscope consists of a single converging lens that produces a magnified image of an object placed near the focal point. The image formed is virtual, erect, and magnified.

- **Magnifying Power of a Simple Microscope:** The magnifying power M of a simple microscope is given by the ratio of the angular size of the image formed by the microscope to the angular size of the object when viewed by the naked eye. It is given by:

$$M = \frac{D}{f}$$

where D is the least distance of distinct vision (usually 25 cm), and f is the focal length of the lens.

Chapter III

Unit III:Electrostatics

2 Marks Questions & Solutions

- **Q1. State Coulomb's Law.**

Ans. Coulomb's law states that the electrostatic force between two point charges is directly proportional to the product of the magnitudes of the charges and inversely proportional to the square of the distance between them. The force acts along the line joining the charges. Mathematically,

$$F = k_e \frac{q_1 q_2}{r^2}$$

where:

- F is the electrostatic force,

- q_1 and q_2 are the magnitudes of the two point charges,

- r is the distance between the charges,

- k_e is Coulomb's constant, $k_e = 9 \times 10^9 \, \text{N m}^2/\text{C}^2$.

- **Q2. What is meant by electric field? Derive the expression for electric field due to a point charge.**

Ans. The electric field (E) is a vector field that represents the force experienced by a unit positive charge placed at a point in space. The electric field due to a point charge Q is given by:

$$E = k_e \frac{|Q|}{r^2}$$

where:

- E is the electric field,

- k_e is Coulomb's constant,

- Q is the point charge,

- r is the distance from the point charge.

- **Q3. Define electric potential and potential difference.**

Ans.

- **Electric Potential:** The electric potential at a point in an electric field is defined as the work done in moving a unit positive charge from infinity to that point without any acceleration. The SI unit of electric potential is volts (V).

- **Potential Difference:** The potential difference between two points in an electric field is the work done in moving a unit positive charge from one point to another. It is given by:

$$V = W/q$$

where W is the work done, and q is the charge moved.

- **Q4. State and explain Gauss's Law.**

Ans. Gauss's law states that the total electric flux through any closed surface is equal to $\frac{1}{\epsilon_0}$ times the total charge enclosed within the surface:

$$\Phi_E = \frac{Q_{\text{enc}}}{\epsilon_0}$$

where:

- Φ_E is the electric flux,

- Q_{enc} is the total charge enclosed within the surface,

- ϵ_0 is the permittivity of free space.

This law is a fundamental tool in electrostatics for calculating the electric field of symmetric charge distributions.

- **Q5. What is a capacitor? Explain its working principle.**

Ans. A capacitor is a device used to store electrical energy in an electric field. It consists of two conductors separated by an insulating material (dielectric). The basic working principle is that when a potential difference is applied across the conductors, charges accumulate on the plates, and an electric field is created between them. The capacitance of the capacitor is defined as the ratio of the charge stored on the plates to the potential difference between them:

$$C = \frac{Q}{V}$$

where:

- C is the capacitance,

- Q is the charge,

- V is the potential difference.

Unit-III (5 Marks Questions & Solutions)

- **Q1. Derive the expression for the electric field due to a uniformly charged infinite plane sheet using Gauss's law.**

Ans.

- **Given:** A uniformly charged infinite plane sheet with surface charge density σ.

- **Solution:** Consider a Gaussian surface in the form of a cylindrical pillbox with one face inside and one face outside the sheet. By symmetry, the electric field due to the sheet is normal to the surface and has the same magnitude on both sides.

  Using Gauss's law:

$$\Phi_E = \oint \vec{E} \cdot d\vec{A} = \frac{Q_{\text{enc}}}{\epsilon_0}$$

  The charge enclosed by the Gaussian surface is $Q_{\text{enc}} = \sigma A$, where A is the area of the pillbox face.

  Since the electric field is uniform and perpendicular to the surface:

$$E \cdot 2A = \frac{\sigma A}{\epsilon_0}$$

Therefore, the electric field is:

$$E = \frac{\sigma}{2\epsilon_0}$$

Thus, the electric field due to an infinite plane sheet of charge is $\frac{\sigma}{2\epsilon_0}$, directed normal to the surface.

- **Q2. Derive the expression for the capacitance of a parallel plate capacitor. Also, calculate the capacitance if the area of the plates is $A = 2\,\text{m}^2$ and the separation between the plates is $d = 1\,\text{mm}$, with a dielectric constant $\kappa = 2.5$.**

Ans.

- **Capacitance of Parallel Plate Capacitor:** The capacitance of a parallel plate capacitor is given by:

$$C = \frac{\kappa \epsilon_0 A}{d}$$

where:

* κ is the dielectric constant,

* ϵ_0 is the permittivity of free space ($\epsilon_0 = 8.854 \times 10^{-12}\,\text{C}^2/\text{N m}^2$),

* A is the area of the plates,

* d is the distance between the plates.

- **Given:**

$$A = 2\,\text{m}^2, \quad d = 1\,\text{mm} = 1 \times 10^{-3}\,\text{m}, \quad \kappa = 2.5$$

- **Solution:** Substituting the values into the capacitance formula:

$$C = \frac{2.5 \times (8.854 \times 10^{-12}) \times 2}{1 \times 10^{-3}} = 4.426 \times 10^{-8}\,\text{F} = 44.26\,\mu\text{F}$$

Thus, the capacitance of the parallel plate capacitor is $44.26\,\mu\text{F}$.

- **Q3. Explain the effect of a dielectric material on the capacitance of a capacitor. What is dielectric breakdown?**

Ans.

- **Effect of Dielectric on Capacitance:** When a dielectric material is placed between the plates of a capacitor, it increases the capacitance by a factor of the dielectric constant κ. The capacitance of the capacitor becomes:

$$C = \frac{\kappa \epsilon_0 A}{d}$$

  The dielectric material reduces the electric field between the plates, which allows the capacitor to store more charge for the same potential difference, thus increasing its capacitance.

- **Dielectric Breakdown:** Dielectric breakdown occurs when the electric field within the dielectric material becomes too large, causing the dielectric to become conductive, leading to a failure of the capacitor. The dielectric breakdown is characterized by the breakdown strength of the material, beyond which it can no longer act as an insulator.

- **Q4. Two capacitors of capacitances 3 μF and 6 μF are connected in series. Calculate the total capacitance of the combination.**

Ans.

  - **Formula for total capacitance in series:** The total capacitance C_{total} for capacitors in series is given by:

$$\frac{1}{C_{\text{total}}} = \frac{1}{C_1} + \frac{1}{C_2}$$

  - **Given:** $C_1 = 3\,\mu\text{F}$, $C_2 = 6\,\mu\text{F}$

  - **Solution:**

$$\frac{1}{C_{\text{total}}} = \frac{1}{3} + \frac{1}{6} = \frac{1}{2}$$

  Therefore:

$$C_{\text{total}} = 2\,\mu\text{F}$$

  Thus, the total capacitance of the combination is $2\,\mu\text{F}$.

Question on Electric Potential and Electric Potential Difference

Question: Explain the concept of electric potential at a point due to a point charge. Derive the expression for electric potential due to a point charge using integration in the x-direction. Additionally, explain electric potential differ-ence and provide the formula.

Answer:

The electric potential at a point is defined as the work done in bringing a unit positive test charge from infinity to that point against the electric field. The electric potential at a point is measured in volts, where 1 volt is the potential when one Joule of work is done in moving a unit positive charge from infinity to that point against the electrostatic force.

Electric Potential Due to a Point Charge:

Consider a positive charge q placed at the origin O, and we need to calculate the electric potential at a point P at distance r from the charge q.

According to the definition of electric potential, the work done to bring a test charge q_0 from infinity to the point P is equal to the electric potential at point P.

The work done in moving a charge q_0 in the electric field is given by the line integral of the electrostatic force:

$$W = \int_{\infty}^{r} \vec{F} \cdot d\vec{x}$$

where $\vec{F}$ is the electrostatic force on the test charge q_0, and $d\vec{x}$ is the infinitesi-mal displacement in the x-direction. The force due to a point charge is given by Coulomb's law:

$$\vec{F} = \frac{1}{4\pi\epsilon_0} \cdot \frac{qq_0}{x^2}\hat{x}$$

For simplicity, we consider the radial direction in 1D, and thus the work done in moving the charge along the x-axis can be written as:

$$W = \int_{\infty}^{r} \frac{1}{4\pi\epsilon_0} \cdot \frac{qq_0}{x^2}dx$$

This integral gives the total work done to move the charge from infinity to point P:

$$W = \frac{1}{4\pi\epsilon_0} \cdot \frac{qq_0}{r}$$

The electric potential at point P is the work done per unit charge:

$$V = \frac{W}{q_0} = \frac{1}{4\pi\epsilon_0} \cdot \frac{q}{r}$$

Thus, the electric potential at a distance r from a point charge q is:

$$V = \frac{1}{4\pi\epsilon_0} \cdot \frac{q}{r} \quad \text{(Equation 3.13)}$$

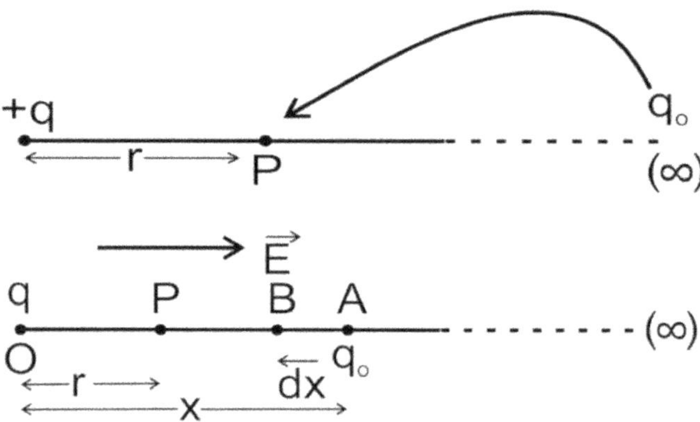

Figure III.1: Electric Potential Due to a Point Charge and Work done in displacing charge

Electric Potential Difference:

The electric potential difference between two points A and B in an electric field is defined as the work done in moving a unit positive charge from point A to point B. The electric potential difference is also known as the voltage between the two points.

The work done in moving the unit charge q_0 from point A to point B in the electric field is given by:

$$W = \int_A^B \vec{F} \cdot d\vec{r}$$

For the potential difference, we consider the change in potential between two points, so the work done in moving the test charge from A to B is:

$$W = \frac{1}{4\pi\epsilon_0} \cdot q_0 \left(\frac{1}{r_B} - \frac{1}{r_A} \right)$$

Thus, the electric potential difference ΔV between points A and B is:

$$\Delta V = V_B - V_A = \frac{1}{4\pi\epsilon_0} \cdot q \left(\frac{1}{r_B} - \frac{1}{r_A} \right)$$

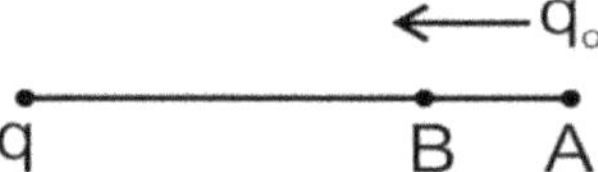

Figure III.2: Electric Potential Difference

Conclusion:

Electric potential is a scalar quantity that represents the amount of work required to move a unit positive test charge from infinity to a specific point in an electric field. The electric potential difference between two points is the work done to move a unit positive charge from one point to another inside the electric field. The expressions for both electric potential and potential difference are derived using the integration method, as shown above.

Chapter IV

Unit-IV :Current Electricity

2 Marks Questions and Solutions

- **Q1. Define electric current and give its unit.**

  Ans. Electric current is the rate of flow of charge through a conductor. The unit of electric current is Ampere (A), which is defined as one coulomb of charge passing through a conductor per second. The SI unit of current is $A = C/s$.

- **Q2. What is resistance? What is its SI unit?**

  Ans. Resistance is the property of a conductor that opposes the flow of electric current through it. The SI unit of resistance is the Ohm (Ω), defined as the resistance when one volt of potential difference causes one ampere of current to flow through the conductor.

- **Q3. State Ohm's Law.**

  Ans. Ohm's Law states that the current (I) flowing through a conductor is directly proportional to the voltage (V) across it and inversely proportional to its resistance (R):
  $$V = IR$$
  where V is the voltage, I is the current, and R is the resistance.

- **Q4. What is the difference between direct current (DC) and alternating current (AC)?**

  Ans.

  - **Direct Current (DC):** The flow of electric charge in one direction only. Example: Battery-powered devices.

  - **Alternating Current (AC):** The flow of electric charge periodically changes direction. Example: Power supply from electric grids.

- **Q5. What is a Wheatstone bridge?**

  Ans. A Wheatstone bridge is a circuit used to measure an unknown resistance by balancing two legs of a bridge circuit. It consists of four resistances arranged in a diamond shape with a galvanometer and a known variable resistor. The resistance of the unknown component is determined when the galvanometer shows zero current (balance condition).

- **Q6. What are the factors affecting the resistance of a wire?**

  Ans. The resistance of a wire depends on the following factors:

  - **Length of the wire (L):** Resistance is directly proportional to the length.

  - **Cross-sectional area (A):** Resistance is inversely proportional to the area.

  - **Material of the wire:** The resistivity (ρ) of the material affects the resistance.

  - **Temperature:** Resistance increases with an increase in temperature for most conductors.

5 Marks Questions and Solutions

Q1. State and explain Kirchhoff's first law.

Ans. Kirchhoff's first law, also known as the junction rule, states that the sum of currents entering a junction is equal to the sum of currents leaving the junction. Mathematically:

$$\sum I_{\text{in}} = \sum I_{\text{out}}$$

This law is based on the conservation of charge. It implies that no charge is lost at the junction; the current is conserved.

Q2. Derive the expression for the equivalent resistance in a series combination of resistors.

Ans. In a series combination of resistors, the total resistance R_{total} is the sum of individual resistances:

$$R_{\text{total}} = R_1 + R_2 + R_3 + \cdots$$

Since the same current flows through all resistors, the total resistance is simply the sum of the resistances.

Q3. Explain the heating effect of current with an example. Also, derive the expression for the heat produced in a resistor.

Ans. The heating effect of electric current is the phenomenon where electrical energy is converted into heat energy when a current passes through a conductor. This effect is commonly observed in electric heaters, toasters, and light bulbs.

The heat produced in a resistor is given by Joule's law:

$$H = I^2 Rt$$

where:

- H is the heat produced,

- I is the current,

- R is the resistance of the conductor,

- t is the time the current flows.

Q4. Two resistors of resistances 4 Ω and 6 Ω are connected in parallel. Find the total resistance of the combination.

Ans. For two resistors in parallel, the total resistance R_{total} is given by:

$$\frac{1}{R_{\text{total}}} = \frac{1}{R_1} + \frac{1}{R_2}$$

Substituting $R_1 = 4\,\Omega$ and $R_2 = 6\,\Omega$:

$$\frac{1}{R_{\text{total}}} = \frac{1}{4} + \frac{1}{6} = \frac{5}{12}$$

Thus:

$$R_{\text{total}} = \frac{12}{5} = 2.4\,\Omega$$

The total resistance of the combination is 2.4 Ω.

Q5. A 2 Ω resistor is connected to a 6V battery. Calculate the current flowing through the resistor using Ohm's law.

Ans. Using Ohm's law:

$$I = \frac{V}{R}$$

where $V = 6\,\text{V}$ and $R = 2\,\Omega$:

$$I = \frac{6}{2} = 3\,\text{A}$$

Thus, the current flowing through the resistor is $3\,\text{A}$.

Q6. What is the terminal potential difference and how does it differ from electromotive force (EMF)?

Ans.

- **Electromotive Force (EMF):** EMF is the potential difference across the terminals of a source when no current is flowing. It represents the energy provided by the source to move a unit charge around a complete circuit.

- **Terminal Potential Difference (V):** The terminal potential difference is the potential difference across the terminals of a source when current is flowing. It is less than the EMF due to the internal resistance of the source.

  The relationship between EMF and terminal potential difference is:

$$V = \text{EMF} - Ir$$

  where r is the internal resistance of the source and I is the current.

Chapter V

Unit V: Electromagnetism

2 Marks Questions and Solutions

Q1. Define magnetic field and its SI unit.

A magnetic field is a region around a magnet or a moving electric charge where the force of magnetism acts. The SI unit of magnetic field strength is the Tesla (T).

Q2. What is meant by magnetic flux? What is its unit?

Magnetic flux is the total magnetic field passing through a given area. It is given by:

$$\Phi_B = \vec{B} \cdot \vec{A} \tag{V.1}$$

The SI unit of magnetic flux is the Weber (Wb).

Q3. Define magnetization.

Magnetization is the vector quantity that represents the magnetic moment per unit volume of a material. It indicates the degree to which a material is magnetized and is measured in A/m.

Q4. Define Lorentz force for a charged particle moving in a magnetic field.

The Lorentz force is the force experienced by a charged particle moving in a magnetic field. It is given by:

$$\vec{F} = q(\vec{v} \times \vec{B}) \tag{V.2}$$

where q is the charge, $\vec{v}$ is the velocity, and $\vec{B}$ is the magnetic field.

Q5. What are the different types of magnetic materials?

Magnetic materials are classified into three types:

- **Diamagnetic materials**: Weakly repelled by a magnetic field. (e.g., Copper, Zinc)

- **Paramagnetic materials**: Weakly attracted by a magnetic field. (e.g., Aluminium, Platinum)

- **Ferromagnetic materials**: Strongly attracted by a magnetic field and retain their magnetism. (e.g., Iron, Nickel, Cobalt)

Q6. State Faraday's Second Law of Electromagnetic Induction.

Faraday's Second Law states that a change in magnetic flux through a coil induces an electromotive force (EMF) in the coil:

$$E = -\frac{d\Phi_B}{dt} \tag{V.3}$$

where Φ_B is the magnetic flux and E is the induced EMF.

Q7. Define Faraday's laws of Electromagnetic Induction.

- **First Law:** Whenever the magnetic flux linked with a closed circuit changes, an EMF is induced in the circuit. The induced EMF persists as long as there is a change in magnetic flux.

- **Second Law:** The magnitude of the induced EMF is proportional to the rate of change of magnetic flux:

$$e = -k\frac{d\Phi}{dt} \tag{V.4}$$

where k is a proportionality constant.

Q8. Define Magnetic intensity and write its SI unit.

Magnetic intensity (H) is given by:

$$H = \frac{B}{\mu_0} \tag{V.5}$$

The SI unit of magnetic intensity is A/m.

Q9. Calculate the Lorentz force acting on a charge.

Given: $q = 2.5C, B = 10A/m, v = 20m/s$

$$F = qvB \sin 90° = 2.5 \times 10 \times 20 = 500N \tag{V.6}$$

Q10. Find the force on a current-carrying conductor.

Given: $l = 0.2m, I = 5A, B = 4A/m, \theta = 45°$

$$F = BIL \sin\theta = 4 \times 5 \times 0.2 \times \sin 45° = 2.8N \tag{V.7}$$

Q11. Magnetic flux through a rectangular loop.

(a) When the plane of the loop is vertical, $\theta = 90°$:

$$\Phi = BA \cos 90° = 0 \tag{V.8}$$

(b) When the plane of the loop is horizontal, $\theta = 0°$:

$$\Phi = 0.60 \times 0.2 \times 0.4 = 4.8 \times 10^{-2} Wb \tag{V.9}$$

Q12. Reduction in deflection of a galvanometer.

Given: $S = 3\Omega, I_g/I = 1/10$

$$\frac{I_g}{I} = \frac{S}{S+G}, \quad 1/10 = \frac{3}{3+G} \Rightarrow G = 27\Omega \tag{V.10}$$

After adding another shunt:

$$S' = \frac{3}{2}, \quad \frac{I_g}{I} = \frac{S'}{S' + G} = \frac{1}{19} \tag{V.11}$$

Q13. Shunt resistance for an ammeter.

Given: $R_g = 10\Omega, I = 10A, I_g = 0.001A$

$$R_s = \frac{R_g}{(I/I_g - 1)} = \frac{10}{9999} \approx 0.001\Omega \tag{V.12}$$

Q14. Path of a charged particle moving perpendicular to a uniform magnetic field.

The particle follows a circular path in a plane perpendicular to the magnetic field due to the Lorentz force acting as a centripetal force.

Q15. Path of a charged particle moving at an angle to a uniform magnetic field.

The particle follows a helical path. The velocity component parallel to the field remains unchanged, while the perpendicular component causes circular motion.

5 Marks Questions & Solutions

Q 1. Explain the principle, construction and working of a moving coil galvanometer.

Ans. A galvanometer is a device for measuring small electrical currents. It is a device that gives a deflection in the magnetic needle whenever the current passes through it. Moving coil galvanometers are the most often used galvanometers for current measurement. It's an electromagnetic device that can detect electric currents as low as a few microamperes.

If a current carrying coil is placed in a magnetic field it experiences magnetic torque. The current through the coil is directly proportional to the angle through which coil is deflected due to magnetic torque.

Construction:

The moving coil galvanometer consists of a rectangular coil made of thin insulated copper wire, wounded on a metallic frame. The rectangular coil is free to rotate about a fixed axis. The coil is suspended freely in a uniform radial magnetic field through a phosphor-bronze strip, connected to a movable torsion head. To make the field radial cylindrical soft iron core is symmetrically positioned inside the coil to improve the strength of the magnetic field. The lower part of the coil is attached to a phosphor-bronze

spring having a small number of turns. The other end of the spring is connected to binding screws. When we pass current in coil there will be oscillation and as per arrangement in this case the oscillation is damped oscillation . The spring is used to produce a counter torque which balances the magnetic torque and hence helps in producing a steady angular deflection. A plane mirror which is attached to the suspension wire, along with a lamp and scale arrangement, is used to measure the deflection of the coil. Zero-point of the scale is at the center.

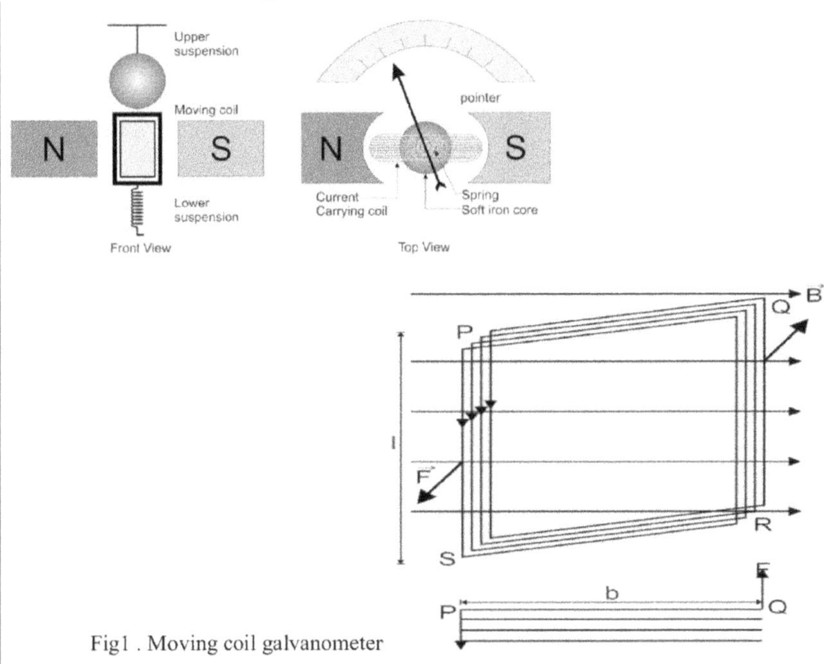

Fig1 . Moving coil galvanometer

Fig.2.Force on rectangular coil in moving coil galvanometer

If a current I flows through a rectangular coil (Fig. 5.2) with a cross-sectional area of A and N turns. The coil receives a torque when it is put in a uniform radial magnetic field B . Consider a single turn 'PQRS' of a rectangular coil with a length of 1 and width of b. This coil is suspended in a

magnetic field with a strength of B, with the coil's plane parallel to the magnetic field. Because the sides PQ and SR are parallel to the magnetic field's direction, as they do not experience any magnetic fields effective force. The sides PS and QR are perpendicular to the direction of field and experience an effective force F given by

$$F = BIL$$

Due to presence of two equal and opposite forces F couple, a couple acts on the coil and produces torque (τ), causes the coil to deflect and the torque acting on ' N " turns of the coil is given by

$$\tau = NIAB$$

The coil rotates because of torque and the phosphor bronze strip twists. In turn, the spring S attached to the coil produces a counter torque or restoring torque $k\theta$ which results in a steady angular deflection. At equilibrium condition:

$$k\theta = NIAB$$

Here k is called as the torsional constant of the spring. The deflection or twist θ is measured as the value indicated on a scale by a pointer which is connected to the suspension wire.

$$\theta = (NAB/k)I$$

Therefore,

$$\theta a I$$

The quantity NAB/k is a constant for a given galvanometer. Hence the deflection in galvanometer is directly proportional to the current that flows through it. The moving coil galvanometer is a highly sensitive instrument and is used to detect the presence of current in any given circuit. The galvanometer can be used to measure: a) the value of current in the circuit by connecting a low resistance in parallel. b) the voltage by connecting high resistance in series.

Q2.   Explain Dia, para and ferromagnetic materials with their properties

Ans.

(a) Diamagnetic materials:

In diamagnetic materials, the atom has no net magnetic moment, because the magnetic moment of each electron is arranged in such a way that they cancel out each other. Such materials are known as diamagnetic materials. These materials are repelled by magnetic field. These materials are also known as negative magnetic materials. The monoatomic (He, Ne, A, etc.) and polyatomic gases (H_2, N_2) and NaCl, diamond, Si, Ge are examples of diamagnetic materials. (b) Paramagnetic materials:

In Paramagnetic materials, the atom has net magnetic moment because of partial cancellation of magnetic moment of individual electrons. Such materials have magnetic moment due to the presence of unpaired electrons. When an external magnetic field is applied, magnetic moment of unpaired electrons align parallel to applied magnetic field, causing a net magnetic moment. The materials with unpaired electrons such as Al, FeO, Oxygen, Titanium, are the examples of paramagnetic materials. (c) Ferromagnetic materials:

In ferromagnetic materials, there is a net magnetic moment due to the presence of unpaired electrons. When an external magnetic field is applied, these magnetic moments are aligned parallel to the applied filed. It results in the increase in magnetization of the materials.

In the non-magnetized state, atomic dipoles in small regions of the ferromagnetic materials called domains are aligned in the same direction (Fig. 1a). The domain exhibits a net magnetic moment even in the absence of external magnetic field. On applying external magnetic field these domains all align themselves in the direction of the applied field (Fig 1.b). In this way, the material is strongly magnetized in a direction parallel to the magnetizing field.

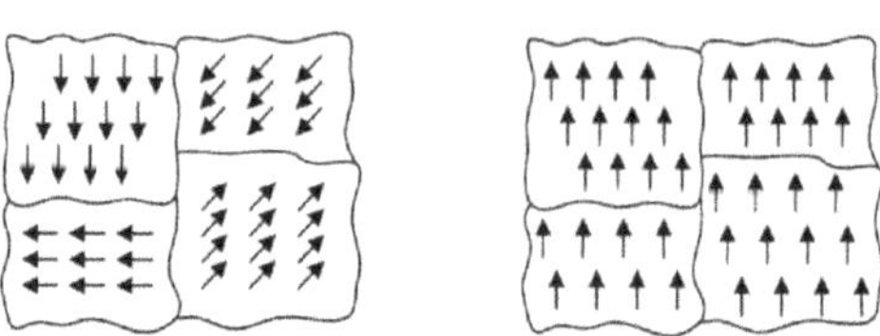

Fig 1. Ferromagnetic materials

Q3.	**Explain Coulomb law of magnetostatics. Draw Magnetic field due to bar magnet.**
Ans.	Consider a bar magnet consisting of magnetic poles (North and South poles) around the end (Figure.1). If we put another bar magnet near to this magnet, there will be force of attraction or repulsion between poles, depending upon the nature of the two poles. The force of attraction or repulsion is directly proportional to the product of the pole strengths of corresponding poles and inversely proportional to the square of the distance between the two poles. This force is also known as Coulomb magnetic force. (like electrostatic force between two charges.)

Mathematically

$$F \quad \alpha \quad m_1 \times m_2$$
$$F \quad \alpha \quad 1/r^2$$
$$F \quad = \quad km_1 m_2 / r^2$$

$k = \mu_0/4\pi = 10^7$ Henry/meter, and m_1 and m_2 in SI unit that is Amp $\times$ m, r in meter and μ_0 is magnetic permeability of free space

An isolated unit positive charges exists, whereas an isolated magnetic pole doesn't exists, but still if we consider an isolated north pole of unit pole strength (m) and kept it at a point ' P ' near to the bar magnet or a current carrying conductor (acting as magnet) then the force on north pole of unit pole strength is the magnetic field due to bar magnet or a current carrying conductor at that point.

$$B \quad = F/m$$
$$\text{Dimensional formula of } B \quad = MLT^2/AL = MA^{-1}T^{-2}$$

The CGS unit of magnetic field is Gauss. The SI unit of magnetic field is Tesla. The magnetic field strength of earth is 3.05×10^{-5} Tesla

$$1 \text{ Tesla } = 10^4 \text{ Gauss}$$

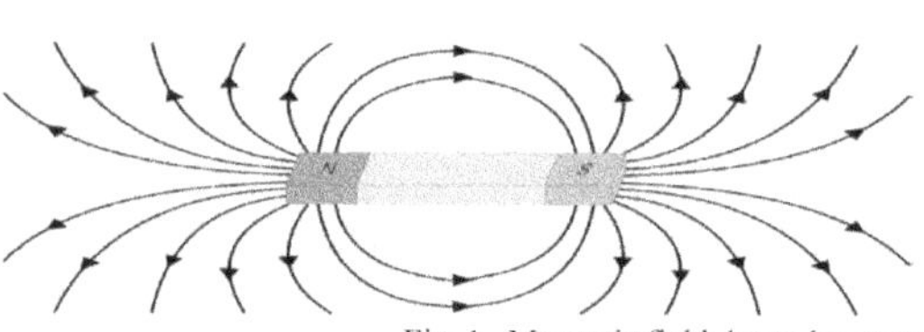

Fig. 1. Magnetic field due to bar magnet

Q4. Define Magnetic lines of force. Write five Properties of Magnetic lines of force.

Ans. The magnetic force existing around the magnet can be explained in terms of the magnetic lines of force (Fig.1). Magnetic field lines originate from the north pole and merge to the south pole of a bar magnet. They do not intersect each other and the strength of the magnetic field is defined as the number of lines of force passing through a unit area perpendicular to the field.

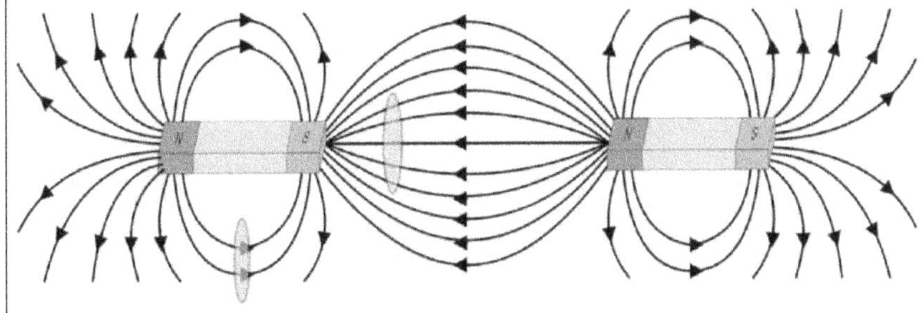

Fig. 1 Magnetic lines of force originating from bar magnet

Five Properties of Magnetic lines of force:

1. Closed Loops - Magnetic field lines always form continuous, closed loops, emerging from the north pole and entering the south pole outside the magnet.

2. No Intersection - Field lines never cross each other, ensuring a unique direction of the magnetic field at every point.

3. Strength Indication - The density of field lines represents the strength of the magnetic field; closer lines indicate a stronger field.

4. Repulsion and Attraction - Field lines exert lateral pressure (like poles repel) and tend to contract (opposite poles attract).

5. Generated by Currents - Magnetic fields arise from moving charges and electric currents, following the right-hand rule.

Q5.   Define Magnetization. Explain Magnetization in details drawing Magnetization curve.

Ans.

Magnetization:

When a magnetic material is placed in a magnetizing field, it gets magnetized. The magnetic moment developed per unit volume in magnetizing material is known as intensity of magnetization of magnetization or Magnetization (I)

$$I = M/V$$

where, V is the volume of the material, with length 2l and area of cross section A
As Magnetic moment m × 2l{m is pole strength and 2l is length of magnet }
We can write magnetization (I) as,

$$I = m \times 2l/V = m/(V/2l) = m/A$$

Thus, magnetization (I) can also be defined as the pole strength per unit area of cross section. The unit of I is Ampere / meter.

Magnetization curve:

The variation of I with H is known as magnetization curve. The diamagnetic, and paramagnetic materials have a linear relation between I and H curve and retain no magnetization when the field is removed. The ferromagnetic materials show nonlinear relationship curve between I and H . At large magnetic field when magnetization becomes constant is known as saturation (I_s). In ferromagnetic materials, I do not reduce to zero when applied field is removed and it is known as retentivity of material (I_R). The field has to be applied in opposite direction to remove the magnetization and this applied field is called coercive magnetic field (H_C).

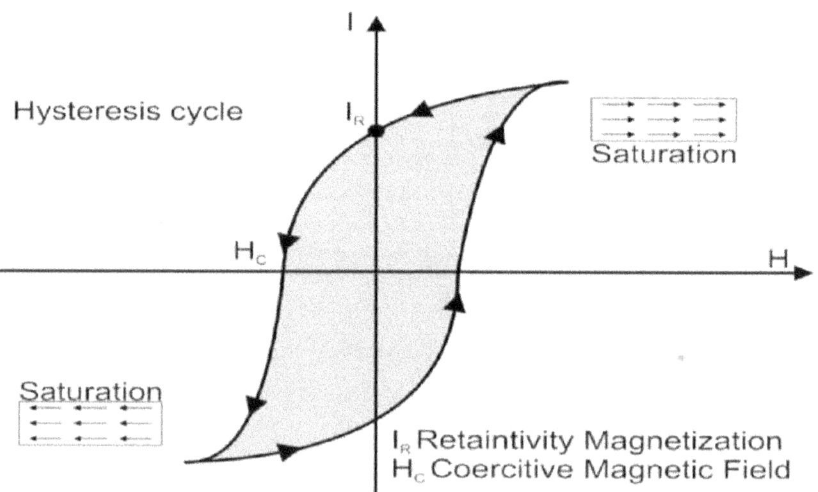

Fig1. Magnetization Curve

Q7. Expain the method of conversion of a galvanometer into ammeter and voltmeter .

Ans Conversion of a galvanometer into ammeter and voltmeter :
Any galvanometer which we get in the market or available in laboratory has two specific parameters. The current Ig for full scale deflection (FSD) and resistance of gal-

vanometer due to resistance of wire of coil. If we know these two parameters, we can convert galvanometer in to ammeter and voltmeter of given desired range.

(i) Conversion of galvanometer into ammeter

A galvanometer is converted into an ammeter by connecting a low resistance called as shunt parallel to galvanometer coil. Shunt resistance is selected as per requirement of the desired range of the ammeter and by connecting shunt the total resistance becomes very low, due to parallel combination of resistances. Ammeter is always connected in series to measure the electric current flowing in the circuit. The current passing though ammeter is divided into two parts: Ig passes through galvanometer coil and remaining current (I - Ig) passes through shunt, as given in Fig. 1. The voltage across the galvanometer and shunt resistance is equal, due to the parallel connection. Therefore, Therefore,

$$GI_g = (I - I)S$$
$$S/G = I_g / (I - I_g)$$

Where, G - Resistance of the galvanometer coil, I - Total current passing through the circuit, I_g - Total current passing through the galvanometer which corresponds to full-scale reading or full-scale deflection, S - Value of shunt resistance.

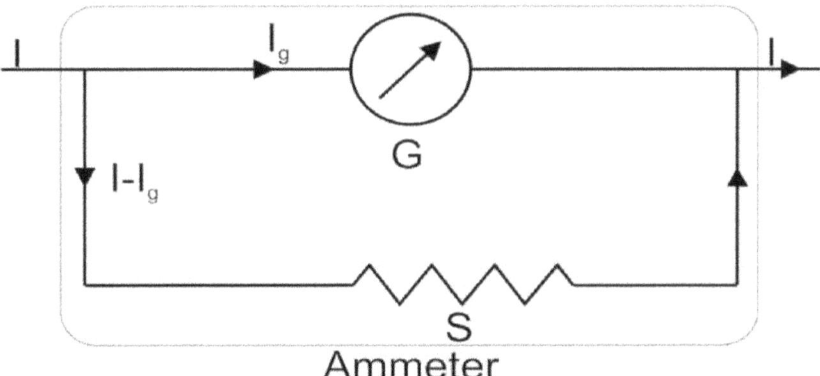

Fig. 1. Conversion of galvanometer into ammeter parallel connection.

Whenever we connect shunt to galvanometer, maximum current passes through the shunt and low current passes through the galvanometer. The deflection in galvanometer is an indication of current in the circuit. The resistance of ammeter is very low and for ideal ammeter the resistance should be zero.

Example: If we have a galvanometer of 25 (I_g) micro ampere FSD and having resistance 15000hm(G). If we have to convert it in to ammeter of 2.5 ampere (I) then the shunt resistance will be,

$$S = G \times I_g/(I - I) = 1500 \times \left(25 \times 10^{-6}\right) / \left(2.5 - 25 \times 10^{-6}\right)$$
$$\Rightarrow S = 1500 \times \left\{ \left(25 \times 10^{-6}\right)/2.5 \right\}$$
$$\Rightarrow S = 15000 \times 10^{-6} = 15 \times 10^{-3} = 15 \text{ milli ohm}$$

(ii) Conversion of galvanometer into voltmeter

A galvanometer is converted into a voltmeter by connecting high resistance in series. As voltage across two parallel point is same, hence voltmeter is always connected in parallel to the component in a given circuit, whose voltage we have to measure. A suitable high resistance is selected, depending on the range of the voltmeter. In the given circuit, G = Resistance of the galvanometer, R = Value of high resistance, I = Total current passing through the circuit, I_G = Total current passing through the galvanometer which corresponds to a full-scale deflection, V = Voltage drops across the series connection of galvanometer and high resistance.

When current I_g passes through the series combination of the galvanometer and the high resistance R; the voltage drop across the branch *ab* is given by:

$$V = G \cdot I_g + R \cdot I_g$$
$$V/I_g = G + R$$
$$R = (V/I) - G$$

The value of R can be obtained using the above equation.

Example: If we have a galvanometer of 25 (I_8) micro ampere FSD and having resistance 1500hm(G). If we have to convert it in to voltmeter of 2.5 Volt(I) then the series resistance will be,

$$R = \left\{ 2.5/\left(25 \times 10^{-6}\right) \right\} - 1500$$
$$R = 100000 - 1500 = 98,5000hm = 98.5 \text{ Kiloohm}$$

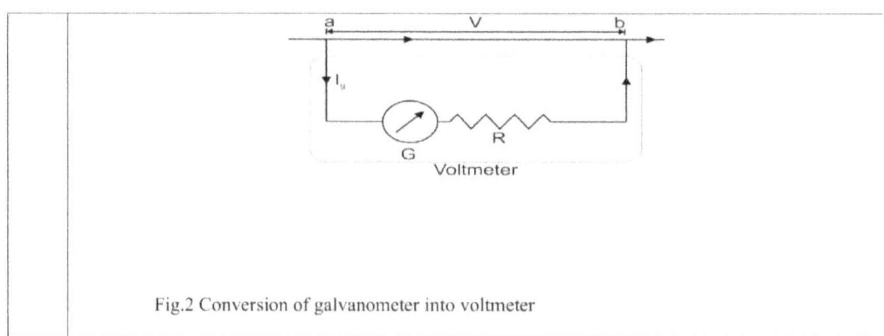

Fig.2 Conversion of galvanometer into voltmeter

Q8. Derive the expression for Force acting on rectangular coil placed in magnetic field.

Force on rectangular coil placed in magnetic field :

Let us consider a current carrying rectangular loop PQRS, placed in magnetic field. The direction of magnetic field and a current loop is such that the normal ($\hat{n}$) to the plane of loop making an angle θ with $\vec{B}$. As described in previous section there will be force in each side of current loop i.e., PQ, QR, RS and SP. Namely F_1, F_2, F_3 and F_4 respectively. For simplicity let us consider that the angle between $\hat{n}$ and $\vec{B}$ is zero then,

$$\vec{F_1} = I(l(-\hat{k}) \times B\hat{j}) = IlB(\hat{i})$$
$$\vec{F_1} = I(l(-\hat{k}) \times B\hat{j}) = IlB(\hat{i})$$
$$\vec{F_3} = I(l(\hat{k}) \times B\hat{j}) = IlB(-\hat{i})$$
$$\vec{F_4} = I(l(-\hat{i}) \times B\hat{j}) = IlB(-\hat{k})$$

Than resultant force on coil is zero and if the angle between $\hat{n}$ and $\vec{B}$ is 90° then,

Fig. 1 Force on rectangular coil placed in magnetic field

$$\vec{F_1} = I(l(\hat{j}) \times B\hat{j}) = 0$$
$$\vec{F_2} = I(l(\hat{i}) \times B\hat{j}) = IlB(\hat{k})$$
$$\vec{F_3} = I(l(\hat{j}) \times B\hat{j}) = 0$$
$$\vec{F_4} = I(l(-\hat{i}) \times B\hat{j}) = IlB(-\hat{k})$$

Hence due to presence of two equal and opposite forces F_2 and F_4 acting in opposite direction a couple acts on the coil and produces torque (τ), causes the coil to deflect and is given by,

$$\tau = \text{Force} \times \text{perpendicular distance between the Forces}$$
$$\tau = IlB \times b$$
$$\tau = I(lb)B = IAB$$

In vector form, $\tau = I(\vec{A} \times \vec{B})$

The force is maximum when area vector $\vec{A}$ (normal to the plane of coil) and $\vec{B}$ are perpendicular, and it decreases as the angle between Area vector and $\vec{B}$ decreases.

Q9. Write the Lorentz force for a moving charge in magnetic field. Predict the trajectory for the angle $\theta = 0$ and 90 degree, where θ is the angle between velocity and magnetic field.

Lorentz force (force on moving charge in magnetic field) :

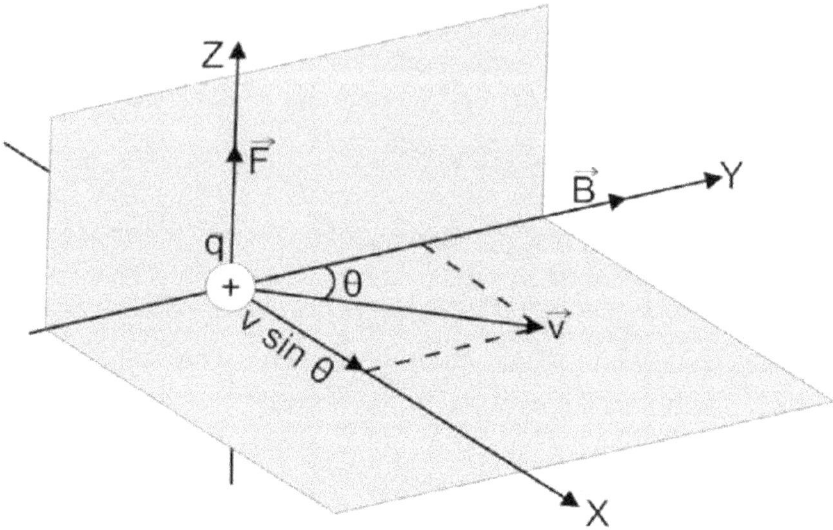

Fig. 1. Force on a moving charge in magnetic field

Let us consider a magnetic field (B) along y direction and a charge (q) moving in xy plane with velocity (v) making an angle θ with the direction of magnetic field. The moving charge will experience a force in the direction perpendicular to motion of charge and magnetic field. This force is known as Lorentz force.

The Lorentz force depends upon following factors

$$
\begin{aligned}
F &\quad \alpha \quad B \\
F &\quad a \quad q \\
F &\quad \alpha \quad v \sin \theta \\
F &\quad = qvB \sin \theta \\
&\quad F = qvB \,(\text{ In case if } \theta \text{ is 90 degree. }) \\
\bar{F} &\quad = q(\vec{v} \times \bar{B})
\end{aligned}
$$

$F \propto v \sin \theta \{ v \sin \theta$ is perpendicular component of velocity $\}$

Case I: If a particle is moving in a direction parallel to magnetic field ($\theta = 0$) then the magnitude of force will be 0 .

Case II: If a particle is moving in a direction perpendicular to magnetic field ($\theta = 90$), then the particle will move in circular path in a plane perpendicular to the direction of magnetic field. Also, if a particle is moving perpendicular to magnetic field than the force only changes the direction of motion of
particle, the magnitude of velocity remain unaltered.

Case III: If a particle is moving in a direction, which is making angle with magnetic field, the particle will move in a helical path.

Q10. Derive the expression for Force on current carrying conductor.

Force on current carrying conductor :

As we know that the rate of flow of charge is current and If the current carrying conductor is kept in magnetic field it will also experience a force. To find the value of that force let us consider a current (I) is flowing is conductor of length (L) and area of cross section (A) with (n) no of charge per unit volume and placed in magnetic field (B). The force due to magnetic field in small length element dl will be given by Lorentz force,

$$dF = qvB\sin(\theta)$$

q is the charge in element $= (nAdl)e$
v is the velocity of electron in element $= v_d$ {drift velocity }
θ is the angle between magnetic field and v_d

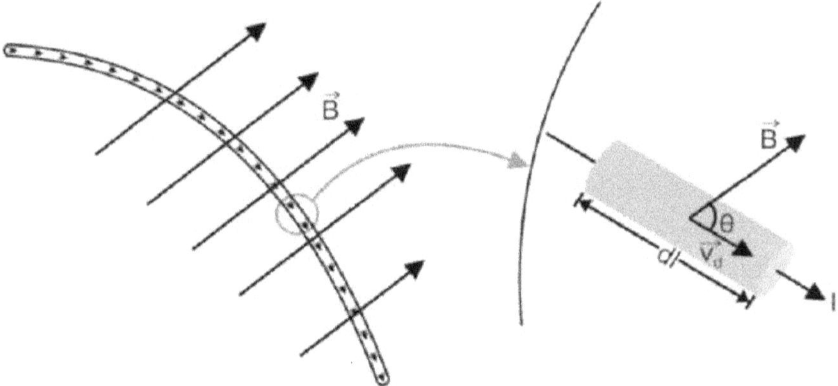

Fig. 1.Force on current carrying conductor
Hence

$$dF = (nAdl)e \times v_d \times B\sin(\theta)$$
$$dF = (nAe \times v_d ddl \times B\sin(\theta)[I = nAevd]$$
$$dF = I \times dl \times B\sin(\theta)$$

on integrating over complete length $\vec{F} = I(\vec{l} \times \vec{B})$

Chapter VI

Unit VI: Semiconductor Physics

2 Marks Questions & Solutions

Q1. Explain the concept of energy bands in solid-state materials.

Ans. Energy bands in solid-state materials refer to ranges of energy levels that electrons can occupy due to the close interaction between atoms in a solid. As individual atomic energy levels overlap, they form continuous bands of energy, which are essential in determining the electrical properties of materials. The main energy bands are:

- **Valence band:** This is the highest occupied energy band containing electrons that are bound to atoms. Electrons in this band are responsible for forming bonds between atoms.

- **Conduction band:** This is the band above the valence band where electrons can move freely and conduct electricity if they have enough energy to reach it.

The separation between the valence band and the conduction band is called the **band gap**, which determines whether a material behaves as a conductor, semiconductor, or insulator.

Q2. How are materials classified based on their conductivity and energy band structure?

Ans. Based on conductivity and energy band structure, materials are classified as follows:

- **Conductors:** These materials have overlapping valence and conduction bands, allowing electrons to move freely with minimal energy input. They have high conductivity, as many electrons are available in the conduction band. Examples include Copper and Silver. Conductivity in conductors decreases with an increase in temperature due to increased electron collisions.

- **Semiconductors:** These materials have a small energy gap (around 1 eV) between the valence band and conduction band. Thermal energy can excite electrons to transition from the valence band to the conduction band, allowing moderate conductivity. Examples include Silicon and Germanium. Conductivity in semiconductors increases with an increase in temperature as more electrons enter the conduction band.

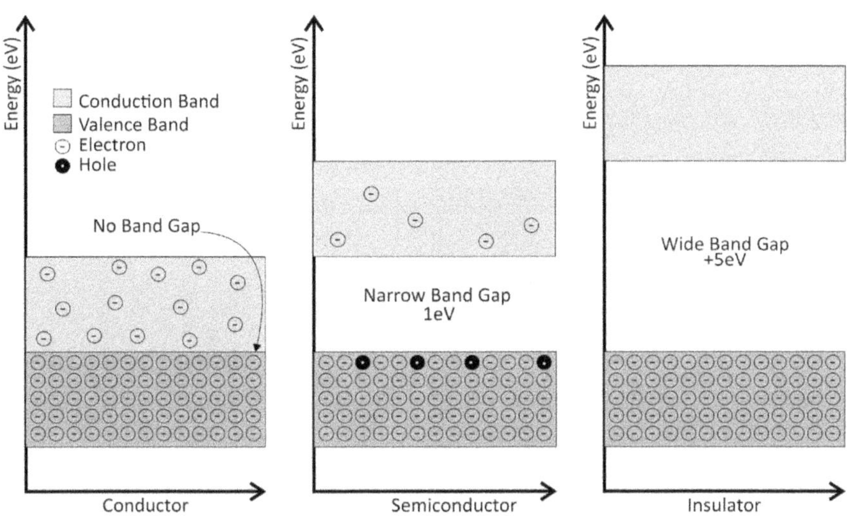

Figure VI.1: Energy band diagram for conductor, semiconductor and insulator

- **Insulators:** These materials have a large energy gap (around 6 eV) between the valence and conduction bands, which makes it difficult for electrons to transition into the conduction band. As a result, they have very low or negligible conductivity. Examples include Rubber and Glass.

Q3. What is the difference between intrinsic and extrinsic semiconductors?

Ans.

- **Intrinsic semiconductors:** Pure semiconductors (e.g., Silicon, Germanium) with no added impurities. The number of charge carriers is equal for both electrons and holes.

- **Extrinsic semiconductors:** Semiconductors doped with impurities to alter their conductivity. They are of two types:

    - **n-type:** Doped with pentavalent elements, providing extra electrons.

    - **p-type:** Doped with trivalent elements, creating "holes."

Q4. What is a p-n junction?

Ans. A p-n junction is formed when a p-type semiconductor and an n-type semiconductor are joined together. It creates a junction with properties that allow current to flow in only one direction, making it the fundamental component in diodes.

Q5. Define the V-I characteristics of a diode.

Ans. The V-I characteristics of a diode describe the relationship between the voltage applied across the diode and the current that flows through it. In the forward bias region, the current increases exponentially with increasing voltage, and in reverse bias, the current is minimal until the breakdown voltage is reached.

Q6. What is the role of a diode in rectification?

Ans. A diode in a rectifier circuit allows current to flow in one direction only, thus converting alternating current (AC) to direct current (DC). In half-wave rectifiers, the diode allows current during only half of the input cycle, while in full-wave rectifiers, current flows during both halves of the input cycle.

5 Marks Questions & Solutions

Q1. Explain the working principle of a p-n junction diode. Discuss its V-I characteristics.

Ans. A p-n junction diode is formed by joining a p-type semiconductor and an n-type semiconductor. The p-type material is doped with acceptor impurities, which create an abundance of holes (positive charge carriers), while the n-type material is doped with donor impurities, creating an abundance of electrons (negative charge carriers). At the junction where these two materials meet, the free electrons from the n-region diffuse into the p-region and recombine with the holes there. Similarly, holes from the p-region diffuse into the n-region and recombine with electrons. This movement of charge carriers leads to the formation of a depletion region around the junction where there are no free charge carriers, only immobile ions.

Formation of Depletion Region and Potential Barrier In the depletion region, due to the recombination of charge carriers, there are immobile positive ions on the n-side and immobile negative ions on the p-side. This forms an electric field directed from the n-region (negative ions) to the p-region (positive ions), creating a potential difference known as the *depletion potential* or *potential barrier*.

This electric field opposes further diffusion of charge carriers. As a result, the diffusion current decreases until it completely ceases when the potential barrier is high enough to prevent the charge carriers from moving across the junction. The potential difference that is created across the junction is typically around 0.7 V for silicon diodes and 0.3 V for germanium diodes, known as the *knee voltage*.

Working of a p-n Junction Diode
The p-n junction diode can be used in two distinct biasing configurations:

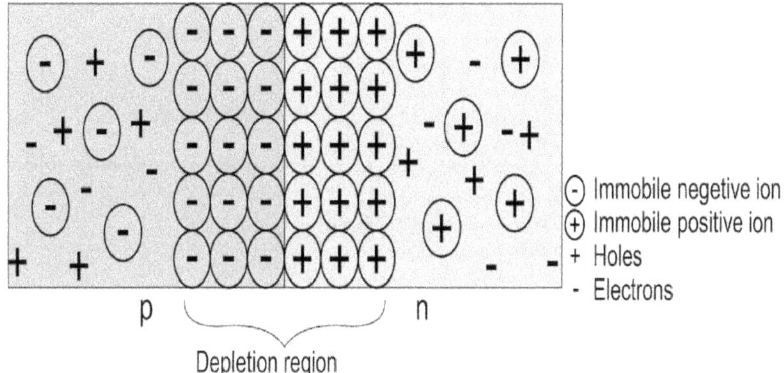

Figure VI.2: Depletion region in pn junction

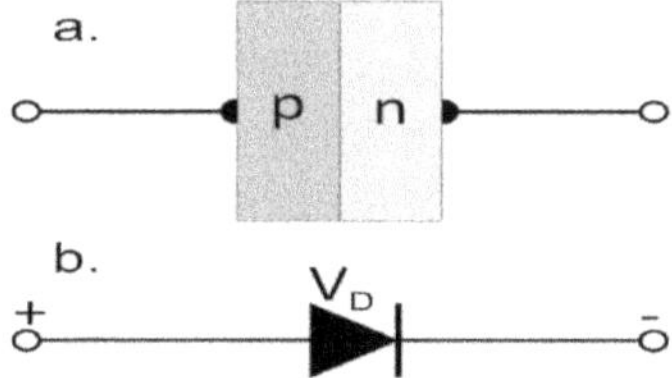

Figure VI.3: pn junction diode and its symbol

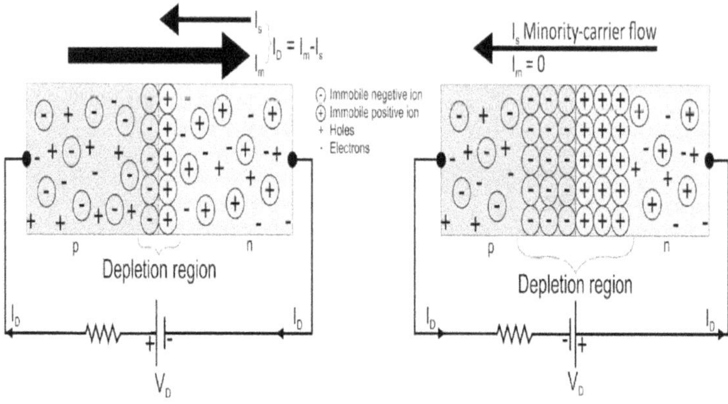

Figure VI.4: Diode in forward and reverse bias

1. Forward Biasing:

In forward bias, the positive terminal of the external power supply is connected to the p-region, and the negative terminal is connected to the n-region. The external voltage opposes the potential barrier, reducing the width of the depletion region and allowing charge carriers (electrons and holes) to cross the junction. When the external voltage exceeds the threshold or knee voltage (around 0.7 V for silicon), the diode starts to conduct, and current flows through the diode. The current increases exponentially with the applied forward voltage.

2. Reverse Biasing:

In reverse bias, the positive terminal of the power supply is connected to the n-region, and the negative terminal is connected to the p-region. This configuration increases the potential barrier and widens the depletion region, preventing the majority charge carriers from crossing the junction. However, a small current, known as the *reverse saturation current* (I_S), due to minority charge carriers (electrons in the p-region and holes in the n-region), still flows. This current is typically very small and remains constant regardless of the reverse bias voltage, up to the breakdown voltage.

V-I Characteristics of a p-n Junction Diode The voltage-current (V-I) characteristics of a p-n junction diode can be divided into two regions based on the applied bias:

1. **Forward Bias Region:** In forward bias, as the applied voltage increases, the current through the diode increases exponentially after the knee voltage (0.7 V

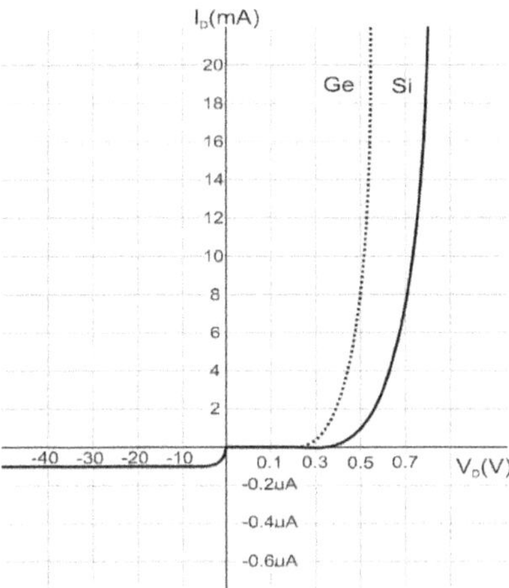

Figure VI.5: Forward and reverse bias characteristics

for silicon or 0.3 V for germanium). The relationship between the voltage and current can be described by the Shockley diode equation:

$$I = I_S \left(e^{\frac{V}{nV_T}} - 1 \right)$$

where I_S is the reverse saturation current, V is the applied voltage, n is the ideality factor (usually close to 1), and V_T is the thermal voltage (approximately 26 mV at room temperature).

2. **Reverse Bias Region:** In reverse bias, the current is extremely small and is almost constant at I_S, known as the reverse saturation current. As the reverse voltage increases, the depletion region widens, but the current remains negligible until the breakdown voltage is reached. At breakdown, the current increases rapidly and the diode may be damaged if not protected.

The ideal V-I characteristics of a p-n junction diode are illustrated as follows:

- In forward bias, for voltages below the knee voltage, the current remains very small (almost zero). Once the voltage exceeds the knee voltage, the current increases exponentially.

- In reverse bias, the current remains constant (at I_S) until breakdown occurs.

Summary:
The p-n junction diode operates based on the movement of charge carriers across the junction, and its ability to conduct current depends on the applied bias voltage.

In forward bias, the diode allows current to flow after the knee voltage is reached, and in reverse bias, the current remains negligible (except for a small reverse saturation current). The V-I characteristics of the diode are exponential in the forward bias and almost flat in the reverse bias, except for the small reverse current.

Q2. Explain the working principle of a half-wave and full-wave rectifier.
Ans.

The supply we receive in our homes is alternating current (AC) supply, also known as AC mains. However, most electronic devices and circuits require direct current (DC) for operation. Therefore, there is a need to convert AC into DC for various applications. This conversion is achieved using a device called a *rectifier*, which uses the properties of a diode. The diode conducts current when forward-biased and blocks current when reverse-biased. Based on this characteristic, different types of rectifiers can be designed.

1. Half-Wave Rectifier:

A half-wave rectifier consists of a single diode connected in series with a load resistance. The AC input is applied to the diode and load resistor. During the positive half-cycle of the AC input, the diode is forward-biased and conducts current, allowing the voltage to pass through to the load resistor. During the negative half-cycle, the diode is reverse-biased and does not conduct current, resulting in no output during that part of the cycle.

Thus, the output of the half-wave rectifier consists of only one-half of the AC input cycle. This produces a pulsating DC voltage, which fluctuates between zero and the peak value of the AC input.

Working of Half-Wave Rectifier:

- A step-down transformer is often used to reduce the AC voltage (e.g., from 220V to 12V).

- The AC signal is given to a circuit where the diode is connected in series with the load resistor (R).

- During the positive half-cycle of AC, the diode is forward-biased and current flows through the load resistor.

- During the negative half-cycle of AC, the diode is reverse-biased and blocks current, causing the voltage across the load resistor to be zero.

The output waveform across the load resistor is a pulsating DC voltage. To smooth out the fluctuations, the output is usually passed through a filter circuit to convert it into a more constant DC voltage.

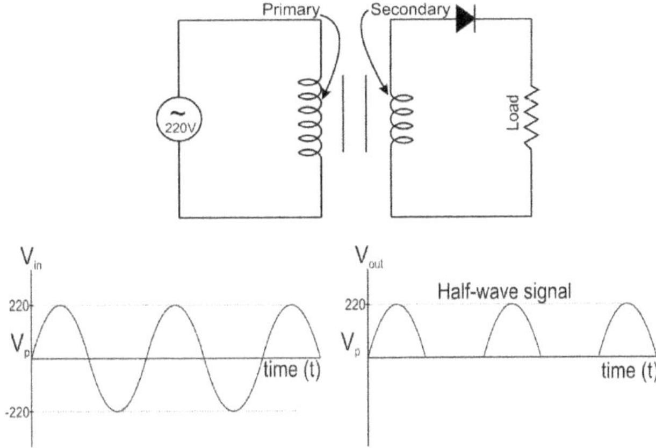

Figure VI.6: Half-Wave Rectifier Circuit and Output Waveform

2. Full-Wave Rectifier:

A full-wave rectifier uses two diodes and a center-tapped transformer to rectify both the positive and negative half-cycles of the AC input. During the positive half-cycle of AC, one diode is forward-biased and conducts current, while the other diode is reverse-biased and does not conduct. During the negative half-cycle, the polarity of the AC supply reverses, causing the second diode to become forward-biased and conduct, while the first diode becomes reverse-biased and blocks current.

Thus, both half-cycles of the AC waveform are utilized to produce a smoother DC output. The result is a full-wave rectified signal, which has a higher average output voltage and is more efficient than a half-wave rectifier.

Working of Full-Wave Rectifier:

- A center-tapped transformer is used, with two diodes connected to the two halves of the AC signal.

- During the positive half-cycle of AC, one diode conducts while the other is reverse-biased.

- During the negative half-cycle of AC, the roles of the diodes reverse, and the second diode conducts while the first one is reverse-biased.

This results in both halves of the AC input being used, producing a smoother DC output. The full-wave rectifier's output is more continuous than the half-wave rectifier, making it more suitable for applications requiring a steady DC voltage.

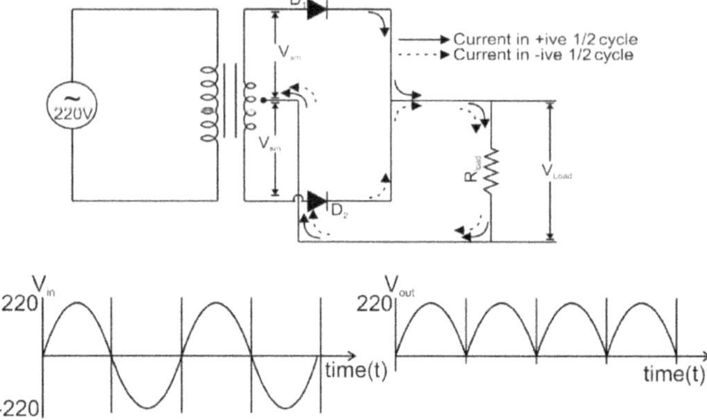

Figure VI.7: Full-Wave Rectifier Circuit and Output Waveform

Comparison of Half-Wave and Full-Wave Rectifiers:

- **Half-Wave Rectifier:**

    - Uses a single diode.

    - Conducts only during one-half of the AC cycle.

    - Output is a pulsating DC with a significant ripple.

    - Less efficient and produces a lower average DC voltage.

- **Full-Wave Rectifier:**

    - Uses two diodes and a center-tapped transformer.

    - Conducts during both half-cycles of the AC input.

    - Output is smoother DC with less ripple compared to the half-wave rectifier.

    - More efficient and produces a higher average DC voltage.

Conclusion:

In summary, a half-wave rectifier allows current to pass through only during one half-cycle of the AC signal, resulting in a pulsating DC output. In contrast, a full-wave rectifier uses both half-cycles of the AC signal, producing a smoother and more continuous DC output. Full-wave rectifiers are more efficient and provide a higher average DC voltage than half-wave rectifiers.

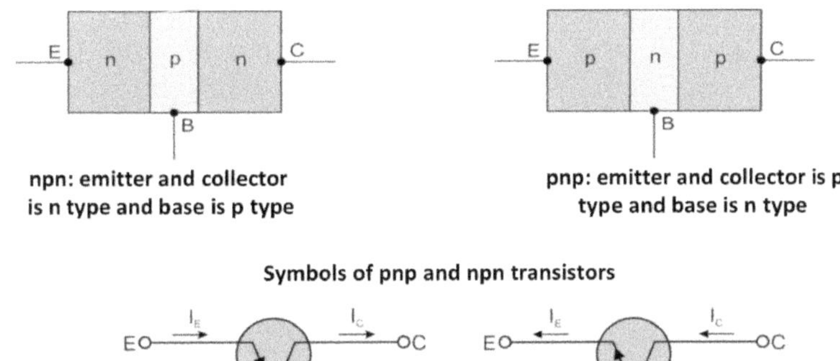

Symbols of pnp and npn transistors

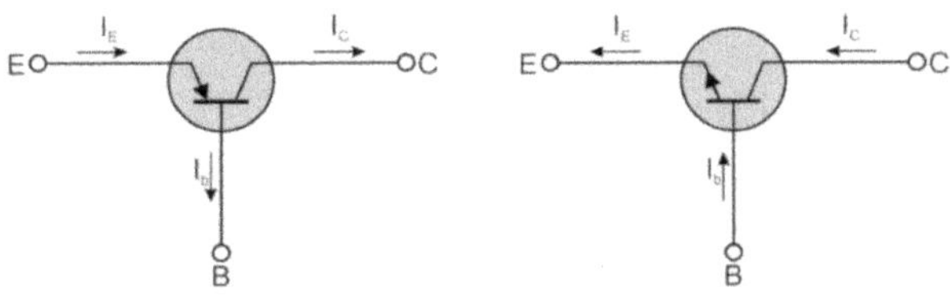

Figure VI.8: npn and pnp transistor and their symbols

Q3. Describe the construction and working of a transistor.

Ans.

A transistor is a three-terminal semiconductor device that is used for amplification and switching applications. It consists of three layers of semiconductor material, and the layers are arranged such that two p-n junctions are formed. The three terminals of a transistor are known as the emitter, base, and collector. Transistors can be classified into two types based on the arrangement of the semiconductor layers:

1. NPN Transistor:

In an NPN transistor, the layers are arranged in the order of n-type, p-type, and n-type semiconductors. The emitter and collector regions are n-type, and the base region is p-type. In this configuration:

- The emitter is heavily doped, while the base is lightly doped.

- The base region is also very thin compared to the emitter and collector regions.

- The emitter-base junction is forward-biased, and the collector-base junction is reverse-biased for normal operation.

In an NPN transistor, current flows from the emitter to the collector, with a small current at the base controlling a larger current between the emitter and collector. The

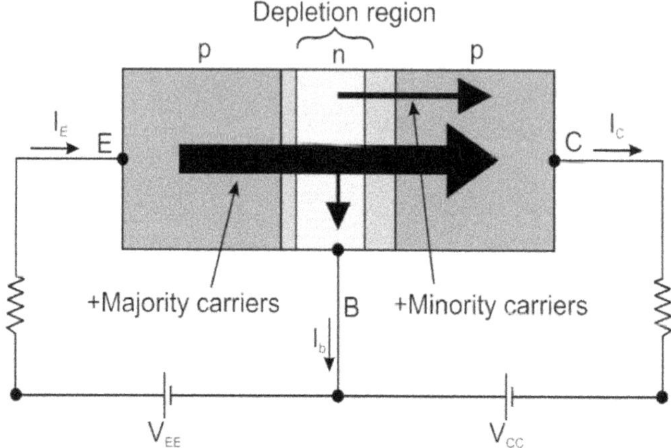

Figure VI.9: Operation of transistor

current that flows from the emitter to the base is very small, and the majority of the emitter current flows through the collector.

2. PNP Transistor:

In a PNP transistor, the layers are arranged in the order of p-type, n-type, and p-type semiconductors. The emitter and collector regions are p-type, and the base region is n-type. The operation of a PNP transistor is similar to that of an NPN transistor, but the direction of current flow is reversed. In a PNP transistor:

- The emitter is p-type and the base is n-type.

- The emitter-base junction is forward-biased, and the collector-base junction is reverse-biased.

- Current flows from the collector to the emitter, with the base current controlling the larger emitter-collector current.

Working of a Transistor:

The transistor operates based on the principle of current amplification. For proper operation, the emitter-base junction is forward-biased, and the collector-base junction is reverse-biased. The key points in the operation of a transistor are:

- When the emitter-base junction is forward-biased, a small current flows from the emitter to the base.

- Since the base is very thin and lightly doped, only a small fraction of the emitter current (the base current) flows through the base region.

- The majority of the current (the emitter current) flows from the emitter to the collector.

- The large voltage across the collector-base junction amplifies the current flowing through the collector.

This phenomenon of amplifying the current is what makes a transistor useful in various electronic applications, such as amplification and switching.

Electronic Applications of Transistors:

Transistors are widely used in many electronic applications, including:

- **Voltage Amplifier:** Transistors can amplify small voltage signals.

- **Current Amplifier:** Transistors can amplify small current signals.

- **Switch:** Transistors are used as switches in digital circuits.

- **Logic Gates:** Transistors are used to design various logic gates for digital circuits.

- **Operational Amplifier:** Transistors are the basic building blocks of operational amplifiers, which are used in signal processing.

Conclusion: A transistor is a crucial component in modern electronics. It operates as a current amplifier and is used extensively in switching applications and signal processing. The NPN and PNP transistors differ in the arrangement of their semiconductor layers, but both follow the same basic principle of operation, with the emitter-base junction forward-biased and the collector-base junction reverse-biased.

Q4. Calculate the output voltage and current for a half-wave rectifier with a peak input voltage of 12 V. Assume the diode has a forward voltage drop of 0.7 V.

Ans. For a half-wave rectifier:

$$V_{\text{DC}} = \frac{V_{\text{peak}}}{\pi} = \frac{12}{\pi} \approx 3.82\,\text{V}$$

The output voltage will be approximately 3.82 V assuming an ideal diode with no losses.

The output current depends on the load resistance R_L. If the load resistance is given, the output current can be calculated using Ohm's Law:

$$I_{\text{DC}} = \frac{V_{\text{DC}}}{R_L}$$

For $R_L = 1000\,\Omega$,

$$I_{\text{DC}} = \frac{3.82}{1000} = 0.00382\,\text{A} = 3.82\,\text{mA}$$

Q5. What are solar cells? Explain their working principle and applications. Answer:

A solar cell is a semiconductor device that converts light energy directly into electrical energy using the photovoltaic effect. When light falls on the semiconductor material (typically silicon), it excites electrons, creating electron-hole pairs. These charge carriers are separated by the built-in electric field of the p-n junction, producing an electric current.

The efficiency of a solar cell depends on the intensity of light and the material used. Solar cells are used in various applications, including:

- Power generation in remote areas,

- Solar panels for homes and businesses,

- Solar-powered devices such as calculators and outdoor lighting.

A solar cell is also a junction device, which is used to convert light energy into electrical energy. The schematic of the solar cell is given in Fig. 6.15. The n-region of the solar cell is thin compared to the p-region, unlike normal p-n junction diodes. This junction is kept in light in such a way that the n-region is exposed to light.

The valence band electrons absorb photons and move into the conduction band. As a result, a large number of free electrons and holes are generated in the n-region. Since the n-layer is very thin, the electric field from the depletion region separates the holes and electrons, forcing the electrons to remain in the n-region and causing the holes to diffuse into the p-region. This results in a positive potential being developed at the p-terminal and a negative potential at the n-terminal. Current flows when an external resistance is added between the p and n terminals.

The voltage developed across the terminals without a load is known as the open-circuit voltage (V_{OC}), which is of the order of 0.5 V. The maximum load current, also known as the short-circuit current (I_{SC}), is of the order of a few mA. This current increases as the intensity of light increases and the absorption of photons in the solar cell increases.

The direction of current inside the solar cell is from the n-region to the p-region, and hence the voltage-current (V-I) characteristics are typically plotted in the fourth quadrant of the graph.

Q.6. Explain the concepts of intrinsic and extrinsic semiconductors. Discuss the characteristics of silicon and germanium as intrinsic semiconductors, the process of doping, and the types of extrinsic semiconductors. Answer:

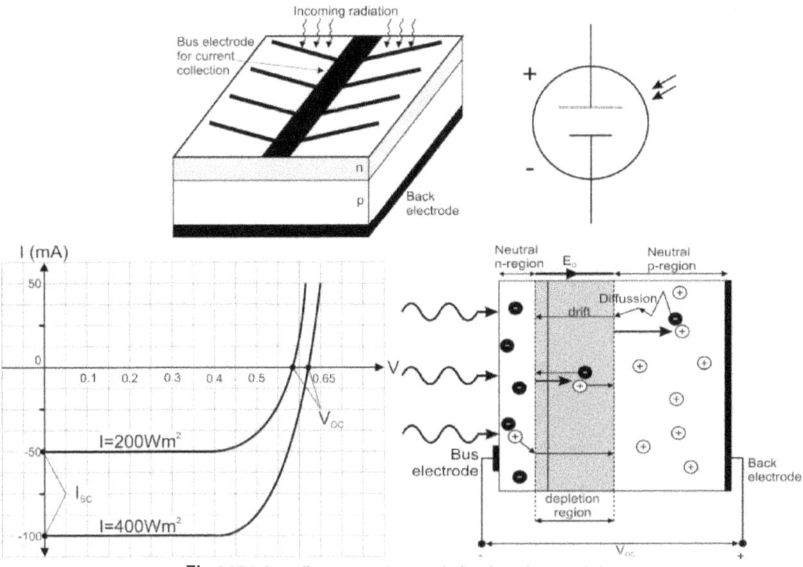

Figure VI.10: Solar cell : construction, symbol and V-I characteristics

Intrinsic Semiconductors: The elements such as silicon (Si) and germanium (Ge) in group IV A of the periodic table are natural semiconductors, known as intrinsic semiconductors. These elements are tetravalent, meaning they have four electrons in their valence shell. In their elemental state, each atom of Si or Ge forms a covalent bond with four neighboring atoms, and there are no free electrons at 0°C. At 0°C, intrinsic semiconductors behave like insulators.

As the temperature increases, thermal excitation causes the covalent bonds to break, and electrons from the valence band transition to the conduction band, leaving behind vacancies known as 'holes' in the valence band. In intrinsic semiconductors, there are two types of mobile charge carriers: electrons and holes. The number of electrons in the conduction band depends on temperature; as the temperature increases, the number of electrons and holes also increases.

The band gap of Si and Ge is 1.12 eV and 0.66 eV, respectively. Germanium is more sensitive to temperature changes than silicon, which is why silicon is preferred in most semiconductor devices. At normal room temperature (300 K or 27°C), the thermal energy of the maximum number of electrons is approximately 0.0026 eV, which is much smaller than the band gap energy. Therefore, only a few electrons can gain enough energy to jump to the conduction band, making the conductivity of semiconductors very low at room temperature.

In intrinsic semiconductors, under thermal equilibrium, the concentration of conducting electrons n and holes p are equal, and their product is given by:

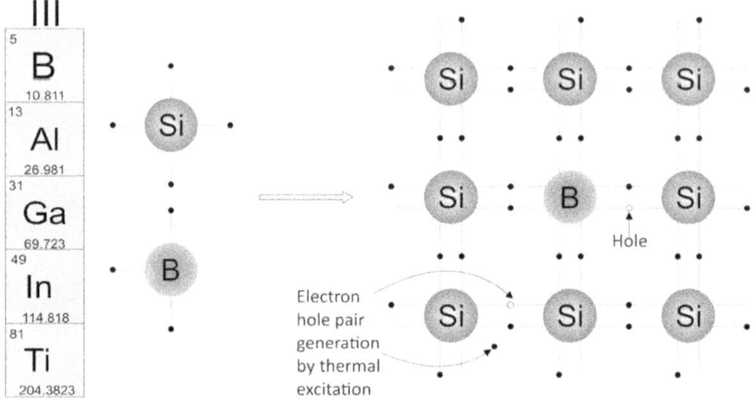

Figure VI.11: p type semiconductor

$$n = p = n_i \quad \text{and} \quad n_i^2 = n \cdot p$$

where n_i is the intrinsic carrier concentration. For silicon at 300 K, $n_i = 1.5 \times 10^{10}$ cm^{-3}.

Since pure semiconductors have very low conductivity at room temperature, it is often necessary to increase the conductivity by introducing impurities. This process is known as doping, and the resulting materials are called extrinsic semiconductors.

Extrinsic Semiconductors: Extrinsic semiconductors are obtained by doping pure semiconductors with other elements to increase their conductivity. The doping concentration is typically very low, about 1 part per million (ppm), meaning one impurity atom is added for every one million atoms of silicon. The dopants can either be from group III or group V of the periodic table.

P-Type Semiconductors: When a trivalent element, such as aluminum, boron, or indium (group III elements), is added as an impurity to a pure semiconductor, it forms a p-type semiconductor. The trivalent impurity atom has three valence electrons and forms covalent bonds with three silicon atoms. The fourth silicon atom's electron remains unpaired, creating a hole. These holes act as the majority charge carriers, while electrons are the minority carriers. The trivalent impurity atoms are known as acceptors because they accept electrons to fill the holes. The semiconductor becomes positively charged due to the majority of holes.

N-Type Semiconductors: When a pentavalent element, such as phosphorus, arsenic, or antimony (group V elements), is added as an impurity, it forms an n-type semiconductor. The pentavalent impurity atom has five valence electrons and forms

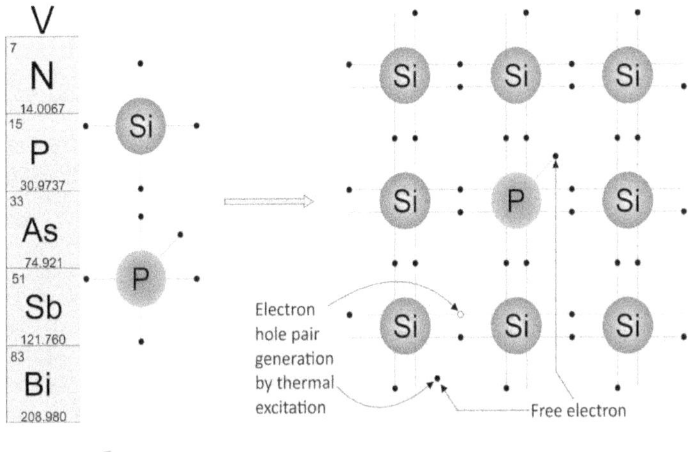

Figure VI.12: n type semiconductor

covalent bonds with four silicon atoms. The fifth electron remains unpaired and is free to move, acting as a majority charge carrier. These impurity atoms are called donors because they donate electrons to the conduction band, leaving behind positively charged immobile ions. In extrinsic semiconductors, under thermal equilibrium, the product of the electron concentration n_o and hole concentration p_o is given by:

$$n_o \cdot p_o = n_i^2$$

In a p-type semiconductor, $p_o \gg n_o$, while in an n-type semiconductor, $n_o \gg p_o$.

Conclusion: Both p-type and n-type semiconductors are electrically neutral overall, meaning the sum of the positive and negative charges is zero. The difference in charge carriers (holes for p-type and electrons for n-type) gives rise to distinct electrical properties, which are fundamental to semiconductor devices.

Q4. Explain the working principle of a photocell and its applications.

Ans.

Photoconductive materials are semiconductors whose conductivity increases in the presence of photons (light). When these materials are exposed to light, the photons are absorbed by the electrons in the valence band, causing them to jump to the conduction band. As a result, the number of free electrons in the conduction band increases, thereby increasing the conductivity of the material. One common example of photoconductive materials is Gallium Arsenide (GaAs).

Photocell:

A *photocell* is a two-terminal semiconductor device that utilizes the principle of photoconductivity. The resistance between the two terminals of the photocell varies with the intensity of the light falling on it. This change in resistance allows the photocell to be used for detecting and controlling light levels.

Construction of a Photocell:

The construction of a photocell involves a thin layer of photoconductive material, such as Cadmium Sulfide (CdS) or Cadmium Selenide (CdSe), deposited onto a ceramic substrate. The photoconductive material does not have a junction like other semiconductor devices (e.g., photodiodes). Two metal terminals are connected at the ends of the photoconductive layer to complete the electrical circuit. The resistance of the material in the absence of light is typically around 100 k. However, when the material is illuminated, its resistance decreases significantly (e.g., it may drop to about 100) due to the increase in the number of free electrons in the conduction band.

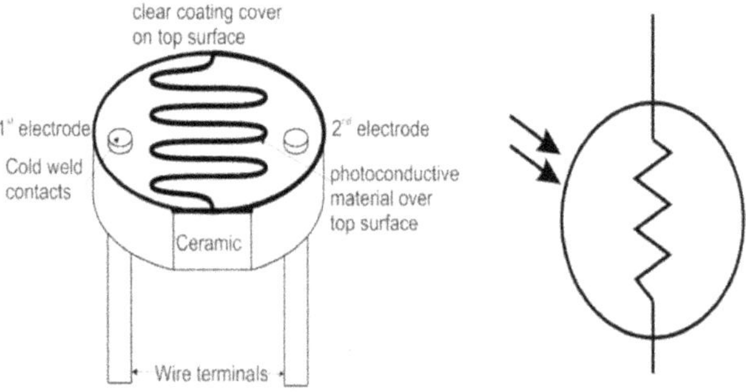

Figure VI.13: Photocell Construction

Working Principle:

In the dark, the photocell behaves like a resistor with high resistance, typically in the range of 100 k. When exposed to light, photons are absorbed by the photoconductive material, exciting electrons from the valence band to the conduction band. This increases the number of charge carriers (electrons) available for conduction, thereby reducing the material's resistance. The greater the intensity of the light, the more electrons are excited, and the lower the resistance becomes. This change in resistance can be used to measure light intensity or control circuits based on the level of illumination.

Applications of Photocells:

Photocells are widely used in various applications where light detection or control is required. Some common applications include:

- **Automatic Headlight Dimmer:** Photocells are used in automatic headlight dimming systems in vehicles. They detect the intensity of light from oncoming traffic and adjust the headlights' brightness accordingly.

- **Night Light Control:** Photocells are used in street lights and garden lights. They automatically turn on the light at dusk and turn it off at dawn, based on the ambient light levels.

- **Street Light Control:** In outdoor lighting systems, photocells can be used to control street lights, ensuring they operate only when the natural light levels are low, such as at night.

Conclusion:

In summary, a photocell operates on the principle of photoconductivity, where the conductivity of a semiconductor material increases in the presence of light. It is used in various light-sensitive applications, including automatic light control systems such as street lights and vehicle headlight dimmers.

Chapter VII

Unit-7 : Modern Physics

Two-Mark Questions and Answers

Lasers

1. **Define ionization potential and excitation potential.**
   Answer: Ionization potential is the energy required to remove an electron from an atom completely. Excitation potential is the energy required to move an electron to a higher energy level within the atom.

2. **Differentiate between spontaneous and stimulated emission of radiation.**
   Answer: Spontaneous emission occurs naturally without external influence, while stimulated emission occurs when an external photon induces the emission of another photon with the same energy, phase, and direction.

3. **What is population inversion, and why is it essential for laser action?**
   Answer: Population inversion is the condition where the number of atoms in an excited state exceeds those in the ground state. It is essential for laser action to achieve amplification of light.

4. **Explain the principle of optical feedback in lasers.**
   Answer: Optical feedback involves reflecting light within a laser cavity using mirrors to enhance the stimulated emission process and sustain lasing action.

5. **Compare the characteristics of Ruby, He-Ne, and Semiconductor lasers.**
   Answer: Ruby lasers use a solid active medium, He-Ne lasers use a gas mixture, and semiconductor lasers use a p-n junction. Their wavelengths differ: Ruby (6943 Å), He-Ne (6328 Å), and semiconductor lasers can vary.

6. **What is a three-level pumping scheme in lasers?**
   Answer: A three-level pumping scheme uses an intermediate energy level to populate the lasing state, with energy supplied by an external source like a flash lamp.

7. **What is the difference between a three-level and a four-level laser system?**

Answer: A three-level laser system requires more energy for population inversion as the ground state is heavily populated, while a four-level system has a lower threshold since the ground state is not directly involved.

8. **What is the active medium in a Ruby laser?**

   Answer: The active medium in a Ruby laser is a crystal of aluminum oxide (Al_2O_3) doped with chromium ions (Cr^{3+}).

9. **State the wavelength of light emitted by He-Ne lasers.**

   Answer: He-Ne lasers emit light with a wavelength of 6328 Å.

10. **What are the engineering applications of lasers?**

    Answer: Lasers are used in cutting, welding, surface treatment, and precision alignment in engineering applications.

11. **What is the medical application of lasers in surgery?**

    Answer: Lasers are used for precision surgeries like LASIK eye surgery and removal of tumors.

12. **What is a semiconductor laser?**

    Answer: A semiconductor laser is a type of laser that uses a p-n junction diode as the active medium and emits light when an electric current passes through it.

13. **List two characteristics of laser light.**

    Answer: Laser light is highly monochromatic and coherent.

14. **What is coherence in the context of lasers?**

    Answer: Coherence refers to the phase uniformity of light waves over time and space, a key feature of laser light.

15. **Explain stimulated emission in terms of photons.**

    Answer: In stimulated emission, an incoming photon causes an excited atom to emit a second photon that is identical in energy, phase, and direction to the incoming photon.

Fiber Optics

1. **Define numerical aperture in optical fibers.**

   Answer: Numerical aperture (NA) is a measure of the light-gathering ability of an optical fiber, defined as $NA = \sqrt{n_1^2 - n_2^2}$, where n_1 and n_2 are the refractive indices of the core and cladding, respectively.

2. **What are the advantages of using optical fibers in telecommunication?**
   Answer: Optical fibers offer higher bandwidth, immunity to electromagnetic interference, lower signal loss, and lightweight construction compared to conventional cables.

3. **Explain the concept of light propagation in an optical fiber.**
   Answer: Light propagates through total internal reflection within the core of the optical fiber due to the refractive index difference between the core and cladding.

4. **Differentiate between single-mode and multi-mode optical fibers.**
   Answer: Single-mode fibers allow only one light path and are used for long distances, while multi-mode fibers allow multiple paths and are used for short distances.

5. **Mention two medical applications of optical fibers.**
   Answer: Optical fibers are used in endoscopy for internal imaging and laser surgeries for precision cutting.

6. **What is the acceptance angle in optical fibers?**
   Answer: The acceptance angle is the maximum angle at which light can enter the fiber and still be guided through total internal reflection.

7. **What is the cladding in an optical fiber?**
   Answer: The cladding is the outer layer of an optical fiber, with a lower refractive index than the core, which ensures total internal reflection.

8. **State two types of optical fibers.**
   Answer: The two types of optical fibers are single-mode fibers and multi-mode fibers.

9. **What is dispersion in optical fibers?**
   Answer: Dispersion in optical fibers is the spreading of light pulses as they travel, leading to signal degradation.

10. **List two sensor applications of optical fibers.**
    Answer: Optical fibers are used in temperature sensors and pressure sensors.

Nanoscience and Nanotechnology

1. **What are nanoparticles? Give one example.**
   Answer: Nanoparticles are particles with dimensions in the nanometer scale (1-100 nm). Example: Gold nanoparticles.

2. **Explain the significance of the surface-to-volume ratio at the nanoscale.**
   Answer: At the nanoscale, the surface-to-volume ratio increases significantly, enhancing surface-dependent properties like catalytic activity and reactivity.

3. **List two properties of nanomaterials that differ from bulk materials.**
   Answer: Nanomaterials exhibit enhanced electrical conductivity and unique optical properties, such as quantum confinement effects.

4. **What is the role of nanotechnology in medical diagnostics?**
   Answer: Nanotechnology enables advanced imaging techniques, like nanoparticle-based contrast agents, and highly sensitive diagnostic tools for detecting diseases.

5. **Name two devices based on nanotechnology.**
   Answer: Nanotechnology-based devices include nanosensors and quantum dots for imaging applications.

6. **What is a quantum dot?**
   Answer: A quantum dot is a nanoparticle that exhibits quantum mechanical properties, such as size-dependent optical and electronic behavior.

7. **Explain how nanotechnology is used in solar cells.**
   Answer: Nanotechnology is used to create thin-film solar cells and enhance the efficiency of light absorption and conversion.

8. **What are carbon nanotubes?**
   Answer: Carbon nanotubes are cylindrical nanostructures made of carbon atoms with excellent mechanical, thermal, and electrical properties.

5-Mark Questions with Detailed Answers

Lasers

(a) **Explain the dual nature of light and how it relates to the concept of photons in lasers.**
   Answer: Light exhibits both wave-like and particle-like behavior, referred to as its dual nature. In the particle picture, light is composed of quanta called photons, each with energy $E = h\nu$, where h is Planck's constant (6.67×10^{-34} J·s) and ν is the frequency. This concept is fundamental in laser operation, as photons emitted via stimulated emission must be coherent and monochromatic.

(b) **Describe the process of spontaneous and stimulated emission with diagrams.**

Answer: - **Spontaneous Emission:** An excited atom returns to its ground state by emitting a photon randomly. The emitted photons have random phases and directions. - **Stimulated Emission:** An incoming photon causes an excited atom to emit a second photon with identical energy, phase, and direction, leading to light amplification.

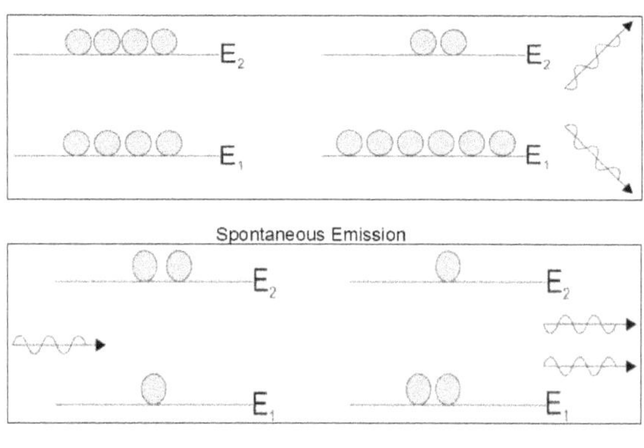

Spontaneous and Stimulated Emission

(c) **What is population inversion? Explain its significance in achieving laser action.**

Answer: Population inversion occurs when the number of atoms in a higher energy state exceeds those in the ground state. It is critical for laser action as it ensures that stimulated emission dominates over absorption, enabling light amplification.

(d) **Discuss the three-level and four-level pumping schemes with suitable diagrams.**

Answer: - **Three-Level Scheme:** Energy is supplied to move atoms from the ground state to a higher energy level, from which they decay to the metastable state where population inversion occurs. - **Four-Level Scheme:** Atoms are excited to a higher energy level and decay rapidly to the lasing level, making population inversion easier to achieve as the ground state remains unpopulated.

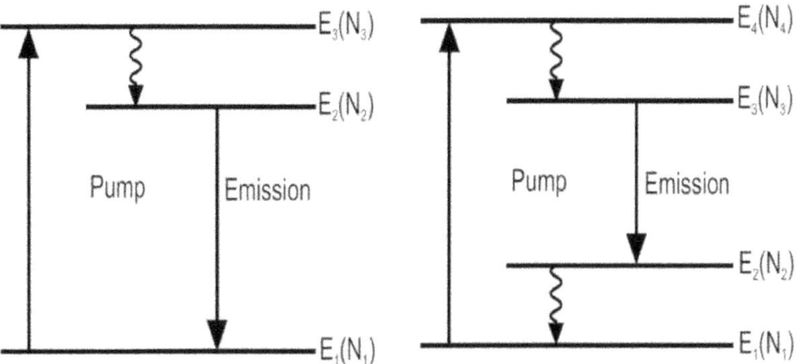

Three-Level and Four-Level Pumping Schemes

(e) Explain the characteristics of laser light. Highlight how these properties make lasers useful in applications.
Answer:

- **Monochromaticity:** Laser light has a single wavelength or color due to the stimulated emission process. - **Applications:** - Precision in spectroscopy for analyzing atomic and molecular structures. - Used in fiber-optic communication to minimize signal distortion. - Barcode scanners rely on monochromatic light for accuracy.

- **Coherence:** The waves in laser light are in phase, maintaining a constant phase relationship. - **Applications:** - Essential in holography for recording and reconstructing 3D images. - Enables interferometry for precise distance and surface measurements. - Stable interference patterns are used in optical testing and alignment.

- **Directionality:** Laser beams are highly directional, with minimal divergence over long distances. - **Applications:** - Used in alignment tools for construction and surveying. - Precision cutting and welding in industrial processes. - Targeting systems and laser pointers benefit from the narrow beam.

- **High Intensity:** Lasers concentrate energy into a narrow, intense beam, resulting in high power density. - **Applications:** - Laser surgery and dermatology utilize high-intensity beams for precision. - Material processing like cutting, engraving, and drilling relies on intense lasers. - Scientific research uses lasers for nuclear fusion and high-energy experiments.

Conclusion: The unique characteristics of laser light—monochromaticity, coherence, directionality, and high intensity—make it highly valuable for diverse applications in science, industry, and medicine.

Fiber Optics

(a) **What are optical fibers? Explain the principle of total internal reflection used in light propagation through fibers.**

Answer: Optical fibers are thin, flexible strands of glass or plastic used to transmit light. Light is guided through the core by total internal reflection due to the higher refractive index of the core compared to the cladding.

Optical Fibers and Total Internal Reflection

Optical Fibers

Optical fibers are thin, flexible strands of glass or plastic used to transmit light. Light is guided through the core by total internal reflection due to the higher refractive index of the core compared to the cladding.

Principle of Total Internal Reflection

The light wave propagates in an optical fiber using the phenomenon of total internal reflection (TIR). This concept has been explained in detail in Unit 2. Figure VII.1 illustrates the representation of light propagation in optical fibers.

Applying Snell's law at the medium-core interface:

$$n_0 \sin \theta_0 = n_1 \sin \theta$$

From Figure VII.1, after substitution for θ, we get:

$$n_0 = 1 \quad \text{(for the initial medium, typically air).}$$

The angle α indicates the light-accepting capability of the optical fiber. For an optical fiber in air, with core refractive index n_1 and cladding refractive index n_2, the acceptance angle α is given by:

$$\sin \alpha = \sqrt{n_1^2 - n_2^2}.$$

The value α is the maximum acceptance angle. If the angle of incidence is less than α, the light wave will propagate through the fiber. Otherwise, it will not undergo TIR and hence cannot propagate through the fiber.

Numerical Aperture

Numerical aperture (NA) is one of the most fundamental characteristics of an optical fiber. It indicates the light-collecting efficiency of an optical fiber:

$$NA = \sin \alpha = \sqrt{n_1^2 - n_2^2}.$$

A higher value of NA indicates better light-collecting efficiency. To maximize NA:

- Increase the core refractive index (n_1).

- Decrease the cladding refractive index (n_2).

Since the core material is typically glass ($n_1 \approx 1.5$), reducing n_2 (ideally to 1) gives the maximum possible NA. However, this effectively removes the cladding, which may not be practical for fiber integrity.

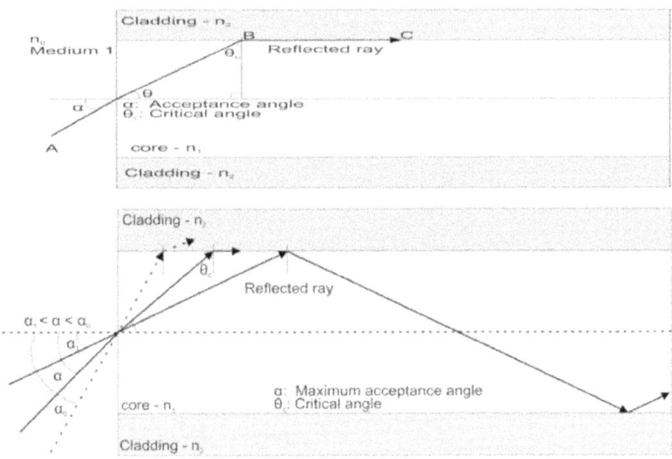

Figure VII.1: Light Propagation in Optical Fibers

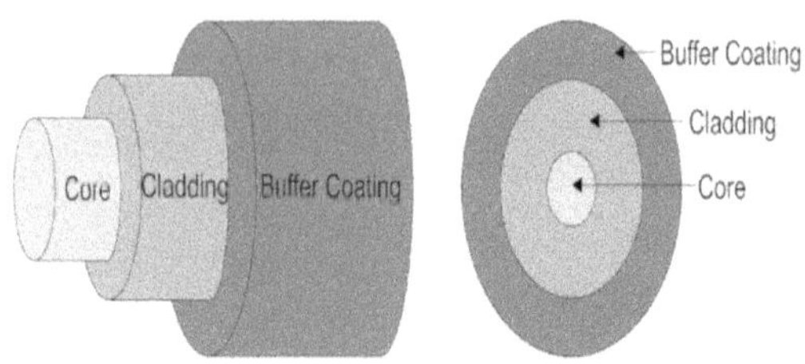

Light Propagation in Optical Fibers

(b) **Define acceptance angle and numerical aperture. How do these parameters affect fiber performance?**

Answer: -**Acceptance Angle:** Maximum angle at which light can enter the fiber and propagate. - **Numerical Aperture (NA):** NA $= \sqrt{n_1^2 - n_2^2}$, where n_1 and n_2 are the refractive indices of the core and cladding. Higher NA allows greater light-gathering ability.

Nanoscience and Nanotechnology

(a) **Explain the unique properties of nanomaterials due to the high surface-to-volume ratio.**

Answer: At the nanoscale, the surface area increases relative to volume, enhancing surface-dependent properties like catalytic activity, reactivity, and strength.

(b) **What are carbon nanotubes? Discuss their properties and applications.**

Answer: Carbon nanotubes are cylindrical nanostructures with remarkable mechanical strength, electrical conductivity, and thermal properties. Applications include nanocomposites, electronics, and energy storage.

Question on Nanotechnology-Based Devices and Nanometer-Sized Devices

Question: Describe in detail the various applications of nanotechnology-based devices, including sensors, solar cells, and batteries. Additionally, explain the concept and working principle of single-electron transistors (SETs) and their significance in nanometer-sized devices.

Answer: Nanotechnology-based devices leverage nanomaterials or operate at nanometer scales. These devices have numerous engineering and medical applications:

- **Sensors:** Nanotechnology-based sensors use components such as carbon nanotubes and zinc oxide nanowires. Due to their nanoscale size, only a few gas molecules are required to alter the electrical properties of the sensing elements, making them highly sensitive. Applications include detecting chemical vapors in industrial and medical fields.

- **Solar Cells:** Nanomaterials like silver nanowires, titanium dioxide nanoparticles, and carbon nanotubes enhance the efficiency of solar cells. For example:

  - Flexible and transparent solar cells use zinc oxide-coated nanowires.

  - Combining carbon nanotubes and buckyballs improves energy conversion rates.

- **Batteries:** Nanoparticles on electrode surfaces increase the surface area, improving power output and reducing charging times. This advancement is critical for high-performance batteries in portable electronics and electric vehicles.

Single-Electron Transistors (SETs): SETs are nanoscale devices that amplify current using controlled electron tunneling. They operate by transferring single electrons across a nanometer-sized gap, utilizing quantum mechanical principles. SETs are significant in low-power electronic circuits and quantum computing due to their precision and minimal energy requirements.

Question on Synthesis and Characterization of Nanomaterials

Question: What is nanotechnology, and how are nanomaterials synthesized? Explain the two approaches for nanomaterial synthesis with examples. Additionally, describe the characterization process of nanomaterials and list the instruments used for it.

Answer: Nanotechnology involves the synthesis (fabrication), characterization (measuring size and properties), and applications of materials with at least one dimension in the nanoscale (1-100 nm).

Synthesis of Nanomaterials:

Nanomaterials can be synthesized using two main approaches:

i. **Top-Down Approach:** This method starts with bulk materials and reduces them to nanoscale dimensions through physical processes. Examples include:

- **Ball Milling:** A high-energy grinding process to break bulk materials into nanoparticles.

- **Mechanical Attrition:** Breaking materials into nanoscale through mechanical force.

ii. **Bottom-Up Approach:** This method builds nanomaterials from atomic or molecular-scale components using chemical processes. Examples include:

- **Chemical Precipitation:** Formation of nanoparticles from solutions.

- **Chemical Vapour Deposition (CVD):** Deposition of thin films or nanostructures through chemical reactions in the vapor phase.

Characterization of Nanomaterials:

After synthesis, nanomaterials undergo characterization to measure their dimensions and properties. This process ensures the desired size and properties of the material have been achieved.

Examples of Instruments Used for Characterization:

- **Scanning Tunneling Microscope (STM):** Used to visualize surface atomic structure.

- **Scanning Electron Microscope (SEM):** Provides high-resolution images of nanomaterial surfaces.

- **Atomic Force Microscope (AFM):** Measures surface topography and nanoscale interactions.

Question on Properties of Nanomaterials

Question: Explain how the properties of nanomaterials differ from their bulk counterparts. Discuss the factors that contribute to these differences, including the roles of surface-to-volume ratio and quantum confinement. Highlight key changes in mechanical, electrical, and optical properties due to size reduction.

Answer: Nanomaterials exhibit properties that are significantly different from those of bulk materials due to their reduced dimensions. These changes arise from the following factors:

Key Properties of Nanomaterials:

i. **Melting Point:** - Nanomaterials exhibit melting point depression, meaning their melting point reduces with decreasing size.

ii. **Lattice Constant:** - The lattice constant of nanoparticles depends on their size and shape, leading to altered crystal structures.

iii. **Mechanical Properties:** - Nanomaterials have higher stiffness and strength. - Carbon nanotubes (CNTs) exhibit fewer defects, resulting in enhanced mechanical performance.

iv. **Electrical Properties:** - Bulk metals may become insulators at the nanoscale. - CNTs exhibit semiconducting or metallic behavior depending on their structure.

v. **Optical Properties:** - Gold nanoparticles appear green due to changes in light absorption and scattering at the nanoscale. - Semiconductor nanoparticles exhibit tunable absorption, which depends on their size.

vi. **Chemical Activity:** - Nanomaterials are more chemically active due to their higher surface energy and smaller size.

Factors Affecting Nanomaterial Properties:

i. **Increased Surface-to-Volume Ratio:** - As the particle size decreases, the surface area increases relative to volume, enhancing properties like reactivity, strength, and electrical characteristics.

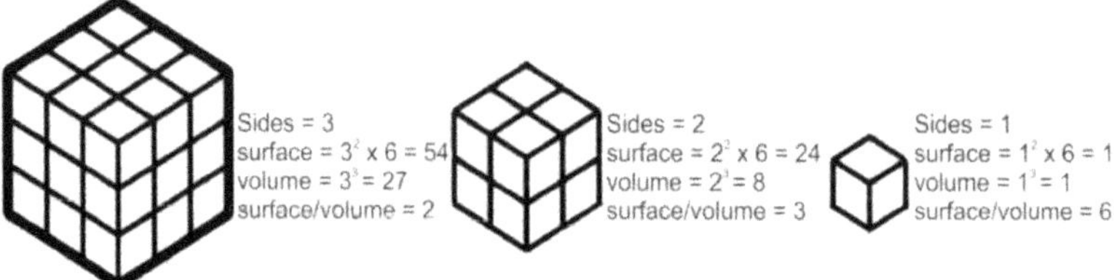

Figure VII.2: Variation of Surface-to-Volume Ratio

ii. **Quantum Confinement Effect:** - Electrons in nanomaterials are confined to a region of nanometer size, leading to discrete energy levels. This phenomenon alters the electronic and optical properties, enhancing features like tunable light absorption.

Conclusion:

Nanomaterials exhibit properties such as reduced melting points, enhanced mechanical strength, tunable optical absorption, and altered electrical characteristics. These differences arise primarily due to the increased surface-to-volume ratio and quantum confinement effects, making nanomaterials highly valuable for applications in various fields.

Question on Applications of Lasers

Question: Discuss the various engineering and medical applications of lasers. Provide examples to illustrate their diverse uses in these fields.

Answer: Lasers have a wide range of applications in both engineering and medicine due to their unique properties, such as coherence, high intensity, and precise control.

Engineering Applications of Lasers:

(a) **Bar Code Readers:** - Laser scanners are used to read barcodes by measuring the light reflected from the white and black lines of the barcode. - This technology is widely used in retail and logistics for quick data entry and inventory management.

(b) **CD/DVD Players:** - A semiconductor diode laser is used to read digital information encoded as "bumps" and "pits" on the surface of CDs or DVDs. - The laser beam reflects off bumps and is absorbed in pits, encoding binary data as variations in reflection.

(c) **Computer Printers:** - Laser printers use a laser beam to create a pattern of text or images on a negatively charged drum. - The areas exposed to the laser attract negatively charged toner, which is transferred to paper and fused to create prints.

(d) **Laser Shows:** - High-power colored lasers are used for entertainment in laser shows to create visually stunning patterns and animations.

(e) **Holography:** - Lasers are used to create three-dimensional images (holograms) by utilizing their coherence property. - Digital holography allows the creation of 3D images of objects or people remotely.

(f) **Position and Motion Control:** - Laser light is used in industrial automation for precise position and motion control systems.

(g) **Fiber Optic Communication:** - Diode lasers convert digital signals into optical signals for transmission through optical fibers. - This is widely used in high-speed telecommunications.

(h) **Material Processing:** - Lasers are used for precise metal cutting and engraving due to their small beam size and high power. - They are also used to create patterns on metal surfaces.

Medical Applications of Lasers:

(a) **Skin and Tissue Removal:** - Infrared lasers are used to remove thin layers of skin (0.1 mm) by targeting water in the skin. - This technique is used for cosmetic procedures and dermatological treatments.

(b) **Laser Hair Removal:** - Laser beams target hair follicles, with the pigment absorbing the light and destroying the follicle, leading to permanent hair removal.

(c) **Retinal Surgery:** - Visible lasers, such as green argon lasers, are used for retinal operations because visible light can be focused on the retina while remaining transparent to the cornea and lens.

(d) **Bloodless Surgery:** - Lasers are used in surgeries to minimize blood loss by precisely cutting tissue and cauterizing blood vessels.

(e) **Cancer Diagnosis:** - Lasers are instrumental in cancer diagnostics, allowing non-invasive or minimally invasive detection techniques.

Conclusion:

Lasers play a vital role in various engineering and medical applications, enabling tasks that require precision, high power, or non-invasive techniques. Their adaptability and efficiency continue to expand their uses in multiple fields.

Question on Laser Characteristics

Question: Discuss the key characteristics of laser light and explain how they differ from ordinary light sources.

Answer: Laser light exhibits several unique characteristics that distinguish it from ordinary light sources. These characteristics include:

Key Characteristics of Laser Light:

(a) **Highly Directional:** Laser light is emitted in a highly directional beam, meaning it travels in a single direction. In contrast, ordinary light sources, such as incandescent bulbs, emit light in all directions.

(b) **Monochromatic:** Laser light is highly monochromatic, meaning it consists of light of a single wavelength. The wavelength spread of laser light is very narrow, typically around 0.01 Å. On the other hand, ordinary white light sources have a much broader wavelength spread, often around 3000 Å, as shown in the figure.

(c) **Coherent:** Laser light is highly coherent, meaning the waves that compose the beam are in phase with each other. This coherence allows for phenomena such as interference and diffraction to be observed with laser light. All the waves within a laser beam oscillate in synchrony, which is not the case for ordinary light.

(d) **Divergence:** The divergence, or angular spread, of a laser beam is extremely small compared to conventional light sources. A laser beam can travel long distances while maintaining almost the same beam size, whereas ordinary light spreads out significantly as it travels.

(e) **High Intensity:** Lasers concentrate energy in a very small region, which results in high intensity. For example, a laser pointer used in a laboratory, even with milliwatt power, can cause eye damage if directly exposed, due to the high concentration of energy in the beam.

Conclusion:

The unique characteristics of laser light, such as high directionality, monochromaticity, coherence, low divergence, and high intensity, make it an ideal source for a wide range of scientific, industrial, and medical applications.

Question on Semiconductor Lasers

Question: Explain the working principle of a semiconductor laser. Describe its active medium, pumping method, and how it operates to produce laser light. Include a diagram of the optical resonator formed in a diode laser.

Answer: A semiconductor laser is a type of laser that uses a p-n junction diode as its active medium. The laser operates by converting electrical energy into light energy, and it is a modified version of the Light Emitting Diode (LED).

Characteristics of Semiconductor Laser:

- **Active Medium:** The active medium is a solid-state material, typically Gallium Arsenide (GaAs), which forms the p-n junction. This material has high doping levels compared to that in LEDs, resulting in a large number of electrons in the conduction band and holes in the valence band.

- **Pumping Method:** The semiconductor laser uses electrical current (forward bias) as the pumping method to provide the energy required for the laser operation.

- **Pumping Scheme:** The energy is supplied through band-to-band transitions in the semiconducting material, where electrons in the conduction band recombine with holes in the valence band, resulting in photon emission.

- **Optical Resonator:** The depletion region at the junction of the p-n diode is cleaved at the ends to form mirrors. These mirrors create a small optical cavity (a few micrometers in size), which traps photons within the junction region. This leads to stimulated emission of light and the amplification of the laser beam.

- **Wavelength:** The wavelength of the emitted laser light is typically around 6328 Å, and it is determined by the energy band gap of the material used in the diode.

Working Principle:

A semiconductor laser works by applying a forward bias to the p-n junction. When the diode is forward biased, the majority charge carriers (electrons in the n-region and holes in the p-region) combine at the junction, releasing energy in the form of photons. The photons are trapped in the optical cavity formed by the cleaved ends of the junction. As these photons reflect back and forth in the cavity, they stimulate the emission of more photons, all traveling in the same direction, which results in the coherent laser beam.

The process of photon emission continues, and the light is amplified until it exits the laser as a beam of coherent light. Although diode lasers generally have less monochromaticity, coherence, and power compared to lasers like the He-Ne laser, their small size and cost-effectiveness make them ideal for a wide range of applications.

Conclusion:

The semiconductor laser is an important device in modern optics, offering a compact and cost-effective solution for generating coherent light. It is widely used in applications such as fiber-optic communication, CD/DVD players, barcode scanners, and more.

Question on He-Ne Laser

Question: Explain the working principle of the He-Ne laser. Describe its active medium, pumping method, optical resonator, and how it produces coherent

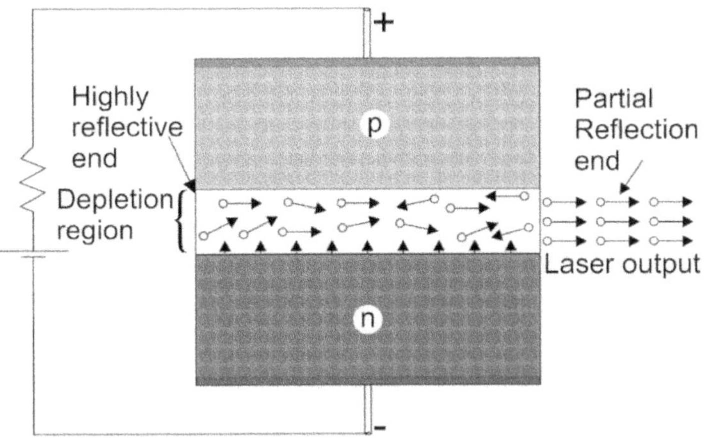

Figure VII.3: Diagram showing the optical resonator of a diode laser. The cleaved ends of the p-n junction form mirrors, creating an optical cavity.

radiation. Include the energy level diagram and construction of the He-Ne laser.

Answer: The He-Ne (Helium-Neon) laser is a gas laser that uses a mixture of helium and neon gases as its active medium. It is one of the most commonly used lasers due to its reliable performance and ease of use.

Key Features of the He-Ne Laser:

- **Active Medium:** The active medium consists of a gas mixture of helium (He) and neon (Ne) in a 10:1 ratio.

- **Pumping Method:** The laser is pumped using an electrical high-frequency signal (electrical discharge) that excites the helium atoms.

- **Pumping Scheme:** The laser uses a four-level pumping scheme where the helium atoms are excited to metastable states (E_2' and E_3').

- **Optical Resonator:** The optical resonator is a quartz tube that contains the gas mixture. Mirrors at both ends of the tube reflect the photons back and forth.

- **Wavelength:** The laser emits light at a wavelength of 6328 Å, which is in the red part of the visible spectrum.

Working Principle:

1. Excitation of Helium Atoms: - The helium atoms are excited to higher energy states (E2' and E3') by collision with high-energy electrons.

2. Energy Transfer to Neon Atoms: - These excited helium atoms then collide elastically with neon atoms in the ground state. Through this collision, the neon atoms are excited to higher energy states (E6 and E4).

3. Photon Emission by Neon Atoms: - The excited neon atoms from states E6 and E4 make transitions to the metastable state E3, emitting photons in the process.

4. *Stimulated Emission: - The emitted photons travel parallel to the axis of the tube. They are reflected back and forth by the mirrors at the ends of the quartz tube. - This reflection process causes further stimulated emission of photons from excited neon atoms, building up coherent radiation within the tube.

5. Laser Output: - As the photons become more intense, a portion of the coherent light escapes from the laser in the form of a laser beam.

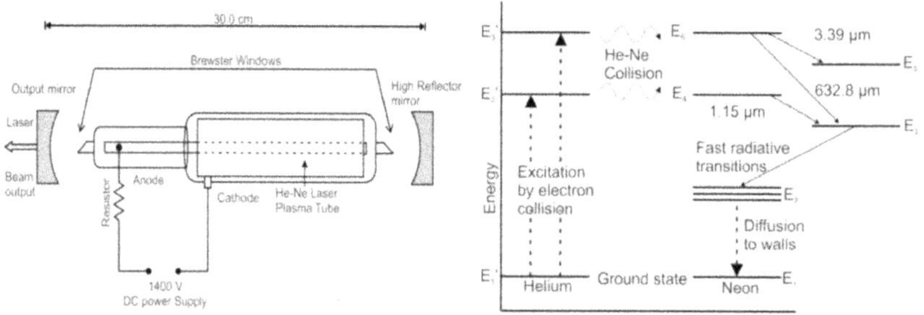

Figure VII.4: Construction of He-Ne Laser and Energy Level Diagram

Energy Level Diagram:

The energy level diagram for the He-Ne laser illustrates the transitions of helium and neon atoms. The energy levels of the helium atoms are depicted on the left, and the neon energy levels are shown on the right. The photons are emitted as the neon atoms drop from excited states (E6 and E4) to the metastable state (E3), leading to the production of coherent radiation.

Conclusion:

The He-Ne laser is widely used due to its stable operation and visible red wavelength of 6328 Å. Its working principle, based on the four-level pumping scheme and energy transfer between helium and neon atoms, makes it an efficient source of coherent light for various applications, including laboratory experiments, barcode scanners, and holography.

Question on Ruby Laser

Question: Explain the working principle of the Ruby laser. Discuss its active medium, pumping method, optical resonator, and how it produces laser light. Include the energy level diagram and construction of the Ruby laser.

Answer: The Ruby laser is one of the first types of solid-state lasers. It uses a synthetic ruby crystal (Al_2O_3) doped with chromium ions (Cr^{3+}) as its active medium. The ruby laser operates using a three-level pumping scheme, and it is known for producing pulsed laser output.

Key Features of the Ruby Laser:

- **Active Medium:** The active medium is a solid-state ruby rod, which is composed of aluminum oxide (Al_2O_3) doped with 0.5

- **Pumping Method:** The laser is pumped using a Xenon flash lamp, which provides a high-intensity light source. The Xenon lamp has a wavelength of around 5500 Å and 4000 Å.

- **Pumping Scheme:** The laser operates using a three-level pumping scheme. The chromium ions are excited from the ground state to higher energy levels (E3 and E4), and from there, they relax to a metastable state (E2).

- **Optical Resonator:** The optical resonator consists of a ruby rod with polished ends that act as mirrors. The mirrors reflect photons traveling through the rod, stimulating further emission of photons, which leads to amplification of the light.

- **Wavelength:** The laser emits light at a wavelength of 6943 Å, which is in the red region of the visible spectrum.

Working Principle:

1.Excitation of Chromium Atoms: - The Xenon flash lamp emits light that excites the chromium ions from the ground state to higher energy states (E_3 and E_4).

2.Relaxation to Metastable State: - The excited chromium atoms relax to a metastable state (E_2), where they accumulate, leading to population inversion between E_2 and E_1 levels.

3. Spontaneous Emission: - Chromium ions in the metastable E_2 state undergo spontaneous emission, emitting photons with a wavelength of 6943 Å.

4.Photon Amplification: - These photons travel through the ruby rod and are reflected by the polished mirrors at the ends of the rod. - Photons traveling parallel to the rod axis are reflected back and forth by the mirrors, stimulating further emissions from atoms in the E_2 state. This leads to the amplification of the laser light.

5.Laser Output: - The process of stimulated emission continues, and an amplified beam of coherent light emerges from the rod. The output is a pulsed laser, not continuous, and the efficiency of the Ruby laser is relatively low.

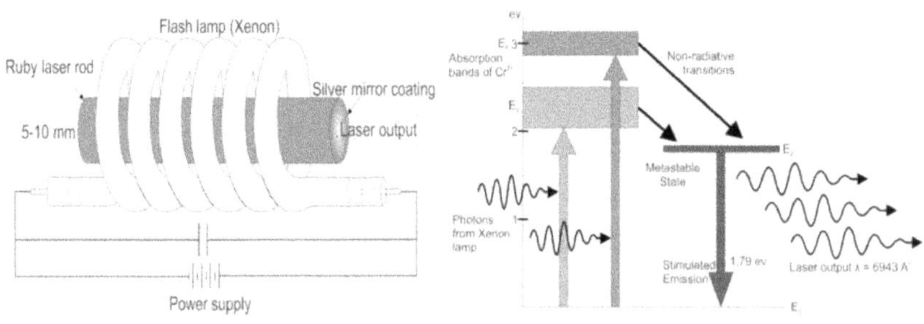

Figure VII.5: Construction of Ruby Laser and Energy Level Diagram

Energy Level Diagram:

The energy level diagram of the Ruby laser shows the transitions of the chromium ions. The Xenon lamp excites the Cr^{3+} ions to higher energy levels (E_3 and E_4). These ions then relax to the metastable state (E_2), where population inversion occurs. The emission of photons from E_2 results in laser light with a wavelength of 6943 Å.

Conclusion:

The Ruby laser is a pulsed laser that uses a three-level pumping scheme and a synthetic ruby rod as its active medium. Although it has low efficiency compared to other lasers, it is historically significant and remains useful in certain applications, such as in research and holography.